CONTENTS

HOMEWORK DIARY	4
EXAM HINTS	5

NUMBER

FRACTIONS	6
PERCENTAGES 1	8
PERCENTAGES 2	10
FRACTIONS, DECIMALS AND PERCENTAGES	12
APPROXIMATIONS AND USING A CALCULATOR	14
RATIO	16
INDICES	18
STANDARD INDEX FORM	20
RECURRING DECIMALS AND SURDS	22
DIRECT AND INVERSE PROPORTION	24
UPPER AND LOWER BOUNDS OF MEASUREMENT	26

ALGEBRA

ALGEBRA 1	28
EQUATIONS	30
EQUATIONS AND INEQUALITIES	32
FURTHER ALGEBRA AND EQUATIONS	34
STRAIGHT LINE GRAPHS	36
CURVED GRAPHS	38
HARDER WORK ON GRAPHS	40
INTERPRETING GRAPHS	42

SHAPE, SPACE AND MEASURES

BEARINGS AND SCALE DRAWINGS	44
TRANSFORMATIONS 1	46
TRANSFORMATIONS 2	48
SIMILARITY AND CONGRUENCY	50
LOCI AND COORDINATES IN 3D	52
ANGLE PROPERTIES OF CIRCLES	54
PYTHAGORAS' THEOREM	56
TRIGONOMETRY 1	58
TRIGONOMETRY 2	60
FURTHER TRIGONOMETRY	62
MEASURES AND MEASUREMENT	64
AREA OF 2D SHAPES	66
VOLUME OF 3D SHAPES	68
FURTHER LENGTH, AREA AND VOLUME	70
VECTORS	72

HANDLING DATA

COLLECTING DATA	74
SCATTER DIAGRAMS AND CORRELATION	76
AVERAGES 1	78
AVERAGES 2	80
CUMULATIVE FREQUENCY GRAPHS	82
HISTOGRAMS	84
PROBABILITY	86

MIXED GCSE-STYLE QUESTIONS — 89

HOMEWORK DIARY

TOPIC	SCORE
Fractions	/29
Percentages 1	/32
Percentages 2	/30
Fractions, Decimals and Percentages	/30
Approximations and Using a Calculator	/31
Ratio	/24
Indices	/45
Standard Index Form	/31
Recurring Decimals and Surds	/43
Direct and Inverse Proportion	/31
Upper and Lower Bounds of Measurement	/28
Algebra	/35
Equations	/38
Equations and Inequalities	/35
Further Algebra and Equations	/34
Straight Line Graphs	/20
Curved Graphs	/24
Harder Work on Graphs	/22
Interpreting Graphs	/23
Bearings and Scale Drawings	/22
Transformations 1	/22
Transformations 2	/21
Similarity and Congruency	/25
Loci and Coordinates in 3D	/20
Angle Properties of Circles	/20
Pythagoras' Theorem	/28
Trigonometry 1	/27
Trigonometry 2	/29
Further Trigonometry	/37
Measures and measurement	/34
Area of 2D Shapes	/30
Volume of 3D Shapes	/29
Further Length, Area and Volume	/26
Vectors	/26
Collecting Data	/18
Scatter Diagrams and Correlation	/21
Averages 1	/29
Averages 2	/22
Cumulative Frequency Graphs	/25
Histograms	/14
Probability	/33

EXAM HINTS

Planning and revising

- Mathematics should be revised actively. You should be doing more than just reading.
- Find out the dates of your first mathematics examination. Make an examination and revision timetable.
- After completing a topic in school, go through the topic again in the GCSE Success Guide. Copy out the main points, results and formulae into a notebook or use a highlighter to emphasise them.
- Try and write out the key points from memory. Check what you have written and see if there are any differences.
- Revise in short bursts of about 30 minutes, followed by a short break.
- Learn facts from your exercise books, notebooks and the Success Guide. Memorise any formula you need to learn.
- Learn with a friend to make it easier and more fun!
- Do the multiple choice and quiz-style questions in this book and check your solutions to see how much you know.
- Once you feel confident that you know the topic, do the GCSE-style questions in this book. Highlight the key words in the question, plan your answer and then go back and check that you have answered the question.
- Make a note of any topics that you do not understand and go back through the notes again.

Different types of questions

- On the GCSE Mathematics papers you will have several types of questions:

  Calculate – In these questions you need to work out the answer. Remember that it is important to show full working out.

  Explain – These questions want you to explain, with a mathematical reason or calculation, what the answer is.

  Show – These questions usually require you to show, with mathematical justification, what the answer is.

  Write down or state – These questions require no explanation or working out.

  Prove – These questions want you to set out a concise logical argument, making the reasons clear.

  Deduce – These questions make use of an earlier answer to establish a result.

On the day

- Follow the instructions on the exam paper. Make sure that you understand what any symbols mean.
- Make sure that you read the question carefully so that you give the answer that an examiner wants.
- Always show your working; you may pick up some marks even if the final answer is wrong.
- Do rough calculations to check your answers and make sure that they are reasonable.
- When carrying out a calculation, do not round the answer until the end, otherwise your final answer will not be as accurate as is needed.
- Lay out your working carefully and concisely. Write down the calculations that you are going to make. You usually get marks for showing a correct method.
- Make your drawings and graphs neat and accurate.
- Know what is on the formula sheet and make sure that you learn those formulas that are not on it.
- If you cannot do a question leave it out and go back to it at the end.
- Keep an eye on the time. Allow enough time to check through your answers.
- If you finish early, check through everything very carefully and try and fill in the gaps.
- Try and write something even if you are not sure about it. Leaving an empty space will score you no marks.

In this book, questions which may be answered with a calculator are marked with 🖩. All the other questions are intended to be answered without the use of a calculator.

Good luck!

FRACTIONS

A Choose just one answer, a, b, c or d.

1. Which one of these fractions is equivalent to $\frac{5}{9}$?
   a) $\frac{16}{27}$
   b) $\frac{9}{18}$
   c) $\frac{25}{45}$
   d) $\frac{21}{36}$ (1 mark)

2. In a class of 24 students, $\frac{3}{8}$ wear glasses. How many students wear glasses?
   a) 9
   b) 6
   c) 3
   d) 12 (1 mark)

3. Work out the answer to $\frac{5}{9} - \frac{1}{3}$
   a) $\frac{1}{3}$
   b) $\frac{2}{9}$
   c) $\frac{4}{6}$
   d) $\frac{4}{12}$ (1 mark)

4. Work out the answer to $\frac{2}{11} \times \frac{7}{9}$
   a) $\frac{14}{11}$
   b) $\frac{14}{9}$
   c) $\frac{14}{99}$
   d) $\frac{2}{99}$ (1 mark)

5. Work out the answer to $\frac{3}{10} \div \frac{2}{5}$
   a) $\frac{3}{4}$
   b) $\frac{6}{50}$
   c) $\frac{6}{15}$
   d) $\frac{4}{3}$ (1 mark)

Score / 5

B Answer all parts of the questions.

1. Work out the answers to the following.
   a) $\frac{2}{9} + \frac{1}{3}$ ....
   b) $\frac{7}{11} - \frac{1}{4}$ ....
   c) $\frac{4}{7} \times \frac{3}{8}$ ....
   d) $\frac{9}{12} \div \frac{1}{4}$ ....
   e) $\frac{5}{7} - \frac{1}{21}$ ....
   f) $\frac{4}{9} + \frac{3}{27}$ ....
   g) $\frac{7}{12} \times 1\frac{1}{2}$ ....
   h) $1\frac{4}{7} \div \frac{7}{12}$ .... (8 marks)

2. Arrange these fractions in order of size, smallest first.
   a) $\frac{2}{3}$ $\frac{4}{5}$ $\frac{1}{7}$ $\frac{3}{4}$ $\frac{1}{2}$ $\frac{3}{10}$

   .... (2 marks)

   b) $\frac{5}{8}$ $\frac{1}{3}$ $\frac{2}{7}$ $\frac{1}{9}$ $\frac{3}{4}$ $\frac{2}{5}$

   .... (2 marks)

3. Decide whether these statements are true or false.
   a) $\frac{4}{5}$ of 20 is bigger than $\frac{6}{7}$ of 14. .... (1 mark)
   b) $\frac{2}{9}$ of 27 is smaller than $\frac{1}{3}$ of 15. .... (1 mark)

4. In a class of 32 pupils, $\frac{1}{8}$ are left-handed. How many students are not left-handed?

   .... (1 mark)

Score / 15

C These are GCSE style questions. Answer all parts of the questions. Show your workings (on separate paper if necessary) and include the correct units in your answers.

1 Gill says 'I've got three fifths of a bottle of orange juice.'

Jonathan says 'I've got two thirds of a bottle of orange juice and my bottle of orange juice is the same size as yours.'

Who has got the most orange juice, Gill or Jonathan? Explain your answer.

....

.... (2 marks)

2 Work out these.

a) $\frac{2}{3} + \frac{4}{5}$ .... (1 mark)

b) $\frac{9}{11} - \frac{1}{3}$ .... (1 mark)

c) $\frac{2}{7} \times \frac{4}{9}$ .... (1 mark)

d) $\frac{3}{10} \div \frac{2}{5}$ .... (1 mark)

3 Charlotte's take home pay is £930. She gives her mother $\frac{1}{3}$ of this and spends $\frac{1}{5}$ of the £930 on going out.

What fraction of the £930 is left? Give your answer as a fraction in its lowest terms.

....

.... (3 marks)

Score / 9

How well did you do?
1–11 marks   Try again
12–18 marks Getting there
19–24 marks Good work
25–29 marks Excellent!

TOTAL SCORE   / 29

For more information on this topic see pages 8–9 of your Success Guide.

PERCENTAGES 1

A Choose just one answer, a, b, c or d.

1. Work out 10% of £850.
   a) £8.50
   b) £0.85
   c) £85
   d) £42.50 (1 mark)

2. Work out 17½% of £60.
   a) £9
   b) £15
   c) £10.50
   d) £12.50 (1 mark)

3. In a survey, 17 people out of 25 said they preferred type A cola. What percentage of people preferred type A cola?
   a) 68%   b) 60%
   c) 72%   d) 75% (1 mark)

4. A CD player costs £60 in a sale after a reduction of 20%. What was the original price of the CD player?
   a) £48
   b) £70
   c) £72
   d) £75 (1 mark)

5. A new car was bought for £15 000. Two years later it was sold for £12 000. What is the percentage loss?
   a) 25%
   b) 20%
   c) 80%
   d) 70% (1 mark)

Score / 5

B Answer all parts of the questions.

1. Work out the answer to the following.

   a) 20% of £60 ....   b) 30% of £150 ....

   c) 5% of £80 ....   d) 12.5% of 40 g .... (4 marks)

2. Colin earns £25 500 a year. This year he has a 3% pay rise. How much per year does Colin now earn?

   £ .... (2 marks)

3. A coat costs £140. In a sale it is reduced to £85. What is the percentage reduction?

   .... % (2 marks)

4. Lucinda scored 58 out of 75 in a test. What percentage did she get?

   .... % (2 marks)

5. The cost for a ticket for a pop concert has risen by 15% to £23. What was the original price of the ticket?

   £ .... (2 marks)

6. The price of a CD player has been reduced by 20% in a sale. It now costs £180. What was the original price?

   £ .... (2 marks)

7. 12 out of 30 people wear glasses. What percentage wear glasses?

   .... % (2 marks)

Score / 16

C These are GCSE style questions. Answer all parts of the questions. Show your workings (on separate paper if necessary) and include the correct units in your answers.

1. The price of a television set is £175 plus VAT. VAT is charged at a rate of 17.5%.

a) Work out the amount of VAT charged.

.... (2 marks)

b) In a sale, normal prices are reduced by 15%. The normal price of a washing machine is £399.

Work out the sale price of the washing machine.

.... (3 marks)

2. A car is bought for £17 900. Two years later it is sold for £14 320. Work out the percentage loss.

.... (3 marks)

3. In a sale, all normal prices are reduced by 18%. In the sale Suki pays £57.40 for a jacket.

Calculate the normal price of the jacket.

.... (3 marks)

Score / 11

How well did you do?
1–7 marks Try again
8–17 marks Getting there
18–26 marks Good work
27–32 marks Excellent!

TOTAL SCORE   / 32

For more information on this topic see pages 12–13 of your Success Guide.

PERCENTAGES 2

A Choose just one answer, a, b, c or d.

1. £2000 is invested in a savings account. Compound interest is paid at 2.1%. How much interest is paid after 2 years?
   a) £4
   b) £5.20
   c) £2.44
   d) £84.88 (1 mark)

2. A bike was bought for £120. Each year it depreciated by 10%. What was the bike worth 2 years later?
   a) £97.20
   b) £98
   c) £216
   d) £110 (1 mark)

3. Roberto has £5 000 in his savings account. Simple interest is paid at 3%. How much does he have in his savings account at the end of the year?
   a) £4 850
   b) £5 010
   c) £5 150
   d) £5 140.50 (1 mark)

4. Lily earns £23 500. National Insurance (NI) is deducted at 9%. How much NI must she pay?
   a) £2 250
   b) £2 115
   c) £2 200
   d) £21 385 (1 mark)

Score / 4

B Answer all parts of the questions.

1. A meal costs £143. VAT at $17\frac{1}{2}$% is added to the price of the meal. What is the final price of the meal?

   £ .... (2 marks)

2. VAT of 5% is added to a gas bill of £72. Find the total amount to be paid.

   £ .... (2 marks)

3. A motorbike is bought for £9 000. Each year it depreciates in value by 12%. Work out the value of the motorbike after 2 years.

   £ .... (2 marks)

4. Scarlett has £6 200 in her savings account. If compound interest is paid at 2.7% p.a., how much interest will she earn after 3 years?

   £ .... (2 marks)

5. A house was bought for £112 000. After the first year the price had increased by 8%, during the second year it increased in price by a further 12%. What is the house now worth?

   £ .... (2 marks)

6. Petrol cost 74.9 pence per litre. The price increased by 2%. Six months later it increased again, by 5%. How much does a litre of petrol now cost?

   .... pence (2 marks)

Score / 12

C These are GCSE style questions. Answer all parts of the questions. Show your workings (on separate paper if necessary) and include the correct units in your answers.

1 a) Work out 40% of £2 500.
....
(2 marks)

b) Find the simple interest on £2 000 invested for 2 years at 4% per year.
....
(3 marks)

2 £7 000 is invested for 3 years at 6% compound interest.

Work out the total interest earned over the three years.

....
(3 marks)

3 Nigel opened an account with £450 at his local bank. After one year, the bank paid him interest. He then had £465.75 in his account.

a) Work out, as a percentage, his local bank's interest rate.

....
(3 marks)

b) Sarah opened an account at the same bank as Nigel. She invested £700 for 2 years at 4% compound interest. How much money did she have in her account after 2 years?

....
(3 marks)

Score   / 14

How well did you do?
1–7 marks   Try again
8–12 marks   Getting there
13–21 marks   Good work
22–30 marks   Excellent!

TOTAL SCORE   / 30

For more information on this topic see pages 14–15 of your Success Guide.

FRACTIONS, DECIMALS AND PERCENTAGES

A Choose just one answer, a, b, c or d.

1. What is $\frac{3}{5}$ as a percentage?
   a) 30%
   b) 25%
   c) 60%
   d) 75% (1 mark)

2. What is $\frac{2}{3}$ written as a decimal?
   a) 0.77
   b) 0.6̇6̇
   c) 0.665
   d) 0.6 (1 mark)

3. What is the smallest value in this list of numbers: 29% 0.4 $\frac{3}{4}$ $\frac{1}{8}$?
   a) 29%
   b) 0.4
   c) $\frac{3}{4}$
   d) $\frac{1}{8}$ (1 mark)

4. What is the largest value in this list of numbers: $\frac{4}{5}$ 80% $\frac{2}{3}$ 0.9?
   a) $\frac{4}{5}$
   b) 80%
   c) $\frac{2}{3}$
   d) 0.9 (1 mark)

5. Change $\frac{5}{8}$ into a decimal.
   a) 0.625
   b) 0.425
   c) 0.125
   d) 0.725 (1 mark)

Score / 5

B Answer all parts of the questions.

1. The table shows equivalent fractions, decimals and percentages. Fill in the gaps.

Fraction	Decimal	Percentage
$\frac{2}{5}$		
		5%
	0.3̇	
	0.04	
		25%
$\frac{1}{8}$		

(2 marks)

2. Put these cards in order of size, smallest first.

   0.31   30% $\frac{3}{8}$ $\frac{1}{3}$ 92% $\frac{1}{2}$ 0.62

   ☐ ☐ ☐ ☐ ☐ ☐ ☐ (6 marks)

3. Decide whether these calculations give the same answer for this question: **Increase £40 by 20%**

   Jack says: Multiply 40 by 1.2

   Hannah says: Work out 10%, double it and then add on to 40

   Explain your reasoning.

   ....
   .... (2 marks)

Score / 10

C These are GCSE style questions. Answer all parts of the questions. Show your workings (on separate paper if necessary) and include the correct units in your answers.

1 Write this list of seven numbers in order of size. Start with the smallest number.

25% $\frac{1}{3}$ 0.27 $\frac{2}{5}$ 0.571   72% $\frac{1}{8}$

.... (3 marks)

2 Philippa is buying a new television. She sees three different advertisements for the same television set.

Ed's Electricals
TV normal price
£250
Sale 10% off

Sheila's Bargains
TV £185 plus
VAT at $17\frac{1}{2}$%

GITA's TV SHOP
Normal price
£290
Sale: $\frac{1}{5}$ off normal price

a) Find the maximum and minimum prices that Bronwen could pay for a television set.

Maximum price = ...

Minimum price = ...   (7 marks)

b) The price of the television in a fourth shop is £235. This includes VAT at $17\frac{1}{2}$%. Work out the cost of the television **before** VAT is added.

.... (3 marks)

3 A sundial is being sold in two different garden centres. The cost of the sundial is £89.99 in both garden centres. Both garden centres have a promotion.

Gardens are Us — Sundial 22% off

Rosebushes — Sundial $\frac{1}{4}$ off

In which garden centre is the sundial the cheapest? Explain your reasoning.

....

.... (2 marks)

Score   / 15

How well did you do?
1–7 marks   Try again
8–13 marks   Getting there
14–22 marks   Good work
23–30 marks   Excellent!

TOTAL SCORE   / 30

For more information on this topic see page 16 of your Success Guide.

APPROXIMATIONS AND USING A CALCULATOR

A
Choose just one answer, a, b, c or d.

1. Estimate the answer to the calculation 27 × 41
   a) 1 107
   b) 1 200
   c) 820
   d) 1 300 (1 mark)

2. A carton of orange juice costs 79p. Estimate the cost of 402 cartons of orange juice.
   a) £350
   b) £250
   c) £400
   d) £320 (1 mark)

3. A school trip is organised. 407 pupils are going on the trip. Each coach seats 50 pupils. Approximately how many coaches are needed?
   a) 12
   b) 5
   c) 8
   d) 10 (1 mark)

4. Estimate the answer to the calculation $\frac{(4.2)^2}{107}$
   a) 16
   b) 1.6
   c) 0.16
   d) 160 (1 mark)

5. Round 5 379 to three significant figures.
   a) 538
   b) 5 370
   c) 537
   d) 5 380 (1 mark)

Score /5

B
Answer all parts of the questions.

1. Decide whether each statement is true or false.
   a) 2.742 rounded to 3 significant figures is 2.74 ....
   b) 2793 rounded to 2 significant figures is 27 ....
   c) 32 046 rounded to 1 significant figure is 40 000 ....
   d) 14.637 rounded to 3 significant figures is 14.6 .... (4 marks)

2. Round each of the numbers in the calculations to 1 significant figure and work out an approximate answer.
   a) $\frac{(32.9)^2}{9.1}$ .... (1 mark)
   b) $\frac{(906 \div 31.4)^2}{7.1 + 2.9}$ .... (1 mark)

3. Work these out on your calculator. Give your answers to 3 s.f.
   a) $\frac{4.2(3.6 + 5.1)}{2 - 1.9}$ ....
   c) $\frac{12^5}{4.3 \times 9.15}$ ....
   b) $6 \times \sqrt{\frac{12.1}{4.2}}$ ....
   d) $\frac{4\cos 30° + 2\sin 60°}{4^3}$ .... (4 marks)

Score /10

C These are GCSE style questions. Answer all parts of the questions. Show your workings (on separate paper if necessary) and include the correct units in your answers.

1 a) Write down two numbers you could use to get an approximate answer to this question.

31 × 79 .... and .... (1 mark)

b) Work out your approximate answer.

....
.... (1 mark)

c) Work out the difference between your approximate answer and the exact answer.

....
....
.... (2 marks)

2 Use your calculator to work out the value of this.

$$\frac{\sqrt{(4.9^2 + 6.3)}}{2.1 \times 0.37}$$

Give your answer correct to 3 significant figures.

.... (3 marks)

3 a) Use your calculator to work out the value of this.

$$\frac{27.1 \times 6.2}{38.2 - 9.9}$$

Write down all the figures on your calculator display.

.... (2 marks)

b) Round each of the numbers in the above calculation to 1 significant figure and obtain an approximate answer.

.... (3 marks)

4 Circle the best estimate for each of these questions.

	A	B	C
a) 52 × 204	700	10 000	1 000
b) 904 ÷ 31	320	30	300
c) 1.279 × 4.9	4	6	8
d) 2795 ÷ 19.1	150	195	102

(4 marks)

Score / 16

How well did you do?
1–11 marks   Try again
12–19 marks   Getting there
20–26 marks   Good work
27–31 marks   Excellent!

TOTAL SCORE   / 31

For more information on this topic see pages 17–19 of your Success Guide.

APPROXIMATIONS AND USING A CALCULATOR

15

RATIO

A
Choose just one answer, a, b, c or d.

1. What is the ratio 6 : 18 written in its simplest form?
   a) 3 : 1
   b) 3 : 9
   c) 1 : 3
   d) 9 : 3 (1 mark)

2. Write the ratio 200 : 500 in the form 1 : n.
   a) 1 : 50
   b) 1 : 5
   c) 1 : 25
   d) 1 : 2.5 (1 mark)

3. If £140 is divided in the ratio 3 : 4, what is the size of the larger share?
   a) £45
   b) £60
   c) £80
   d) £90 (1 mark)

4. A recipe for 4 people needs 800 g of flour. How much flour is needed for 6 people?
   a) 12 g
   b) 120 g
   c) 12 kg
   d) 1200 g (1 mark)

5. If 9 oranges cost £1.08, how much would 14 similar oranges cost?
   a) £1.50
   b) £1.68
   c) £1.20
   d) £1.84 (1 mark)

Score / 5

B
Answer all parts of the questions.

1. Write down each of the following ratios in the form 1 : n.

   a) 10 : 15 .... (1 mark)

   b) 6 : 10 .... (1 mark)

   c) 9 : 27 .... (1 mark)

2. Seven bottles of lemonade have a total capacity of 1680 ml. Work out the total capacity for five similar bottles.

   .... m (1 mark)

3. a) Increase £4.10 in the ratio 2 : 5 .... (1 mark)

   b) Decrease 120 g in the ratio 5 : 2 .... (1 mark)

4. Mrs London inherited £55 000. She divided the money between her children in the ratio 3 : 3 : 5. How much did the child with the largest share receive?

   £ .... (2 marks)

5. It takes 6 men 3 days to dig and lay a cable. How long would it take 4 men?

   .... days (2 marks)

Score / 10

C These are GCSE style questions. Answer all parts of the questions. Show your workings (on separate paper if necessary) and include the correct units in your answers.

1 Vicky and Tracy share £14 400 in the ratio 4 : 5. Work out how much each of them receives.

Vicky: £ .... Tracy: £ .... (3 marks)

2 James uses these ingredients to make 12 buns.

50 g butter
40 g sugar
2 eggs
45 g flour
15 ml milk

James wants to make 18 similar buns. Write down how much of each ingredient he needs for 18 buns.

butter .... g   sugar .... g

eggs ....   flour .... g

milk .... ml   (3 marks)

3 It takes 3 builders 16 days to build a wall. All the builders work at the same rate.

How long would it take 8 builders to build a wall the same size?

.... days   (3 marks)

Score   / 9

How well did you do?
1–6 marks Try again
7–11 marks Getting there
12–17 marks Good work
18–24 marks Excellent!

TOTAL SCORE   /24

For more information on this topic see pages 20–21 of your Success Guide.

INDICES

A Choose just one answer, a, b, c or d.

1. In index form, what is the value of $8^3 \times 8^{11}$?
   a) 8^{14}
   b) 8^{33}
   c) 64^{14}
   d) 64^{33} (1 mark)

2. In index form, what is the value of $(4^2)^3$?
   a) 12^2
   b) 4^5
   c) 4^6
   d) 16^6 (1 mark)

3. What is the value of 5^0?
   a) 5
   b) 0
   c) 25
   d) 1 (1 mark)

4. What is the value of 5^{-2}?
   a) $\frac{1}{25}$
   b) -5
   c) 25
   d) -25 (1 mark)

5. What is the value of $7^{-12} \div 7^{+2}$ written in index form?
   a) 7^{10}
   b) 7^{-14}
   c) 7^{14}
   d) 7^{-10} (1 mark)

Score / 5

B Answer all parts of the questions.

1. Decide whether each of these expressions is true or false.   True   False
   a) $a^4 \times a^5 = a^{20}$ ☐ ☐ (1 mark)
   b) $2a^4 \times 3a^2 = 5a^8$ ☐ ☐ (1 mark)
   c) $10a^6 \div 2a^4 = 5a^2$ ☐ ☐ (1 mark)
   d) $20a^4b^2 \div 10a^5b = 2a^{-1}b$ ☐ ☐ (1 mark)
   e) $(2a^3)^3 = 6a^9$ ☐ ☐ (1 mark)
   f) $4^0 = 1$ ☐ ☐ (1 mark)

2. Simplify the following expressions.
   a) $(5a)^0 =$ ....
   b) $(2a^2)^4 =$ ....
   c) $12a^4 \div 16a^7 =$ ....
   d) $(3a^2b^3)^3 =$ .... (4 marks)

3. Write these using negative indices.
   a) $\frac{4}{x^2} =$ ....
   b) $\frac{a^2}{b^3} =$ ....
   c) $\frac{3}{y^5} =$ .... (3 marks)

4. Evaluate these expressions.
   a) $25^{-\frac{1}{2}}$
   b) $49^{\frac{3}{2}}$
   c) $\left(\frac{4}{5}\right)^{-2}$
   d) $81^{\frac{3}{4}}$

   .... (4 marks)

Score / 17

C These are GCSE style questions. Answer all parts of the questions. Show your workings (on separate paper if necessary) and include the correct units in your answers.

1 Simplify these.

a) $p^3 \times p^4$ .... (1 mark)

b) $\dfrac{n^3}{n^7}$ .... (1 mark)

c) $\dfrac{a^3 \times a^4}{a}$ .... (1 mark)

d) $\dfrac{12a^2b}{3a}$ .... (1 mark)

2 Work out these.

a) 3^0 .... b) 5^{-2} .... c) $3^4 \times 2^3$ ....

d) $64^{\frac{2}{3}}$ .... e) $125^{-\frac{1}{3}}$ .... (5 marks)

3 a) Evaluate the following.

i) 8^0 .... (1 mark)

ii) 4^{-2} .... (1 mark)

iii) $\dfrac{4}{9}^{-\frac{1}{2}}$ .... (1 mark)

b) Write this as a single power of 5.

$\dfrac{5^7 \times 5^3}{(5^2)^3}$ .... (2 marks)

4 Evaluate the following, giving your answers as fractions.

a) 5^{-3} .... (1 mark)

b) $\left(\dfrac{2}{3}\right)^{-2}$ .... (1 mark)

c) $(8)^{-\frac{2}{3}}$ .... (1 mark)

5 Simplify these, leaving your answer in the form 2^n.

a) $4^{-\frac{1}{2}}$ .... (1 mark)

b) $\dfrac{2^7 \times 2^9}{2^{-4}}$ .... (1 mark)

c) $(\sqrt{2})^5$ .... (1 mark)

6 Simplify these expressions.

a) $(5x)^{-3}$ b) $(2x^2y^3)^{-4}$ c) $(3y)^{-3}$

....   (3 marks)

Score   / 23

How well did you do?
1–12 marks   Try again
13–23 marks Getting there
24–34 marks Good work
35–45 marks Excellent!

TOTAL SCORE   / 45

For more information on this topic see pages 22–23 of your Success Guide.

STANDARD INDEX FORM

A Choose just one answer, a, b, c or d.

1 What is this number written in standard form?   42 710
   a) 42.71×10^3
   b) 4.271×10^4
   c) 4271.0×10
   d) 427.1×10^2 (1 mark)

2 What is 6.4×10^{-3} written as an ordinary number?
   a) 6400
   b) 0.0064
   c) 64
   d) 0.064 (1 mark)

3 What is 2.7×10^4 written as an ordinary number?
   a) 27 000   b) 0.27
   c) 270   d) 0.000 27 (1 mark)

4 What would $(4 \times 10^9) \times (2 \times 10^6)$ worked out and written in standard form be?
   a) 8×10^{54}
   b) 8×10^{15}
   c) 8×10^3
   d) 6×10^{15} (1 mark)

5 What would $(3 \times 10^4)^2$ worked out and written in standard form be?
   a) 9×10^6
   b) 9×10^8
   c) 9×10^9
   d) 3×10^8 (1 mark)

Score   / 5

B Answer all parts of the questions.

1 Decide whether each of the statements is true or false.
   a) 4710 is 4.71×10^3 written in standard form. .... (1 mark)
   b) 249 000 is 24.9×10^4 written in standard form. .... (1 mark)
   c) 0.047 is 47×10^{-3} written in standard form. .... (1 mark)
   d) 0.000 009 6 is 9.6×10^{-7} written in standard form. .... (1 mark)

2 Carry out the following calculations. Give your answer in standard form.
   a) $(4 \times 10^6) \times (2 \times 10^9)$ .... (1 mark)
   b) $(7 \times 10^{-3}) \times (2 \times 10^6)$ .... (1 mark)
   c) $(9 \times 10^{12}) \div (3 \times 10^{-4})$ .... (1 mark)
   d) $(2.4 \times 10^{10}) \div (3 \times 10^6)$ .... (1 mark)

3 Work out these calculations. Give your answer in standard form.
   a) $(2.1 \times 10^7) \times (3.9 \times 10^{-4})$ .... (1 mark)
   b) $(6.3 \times 10^{-4}) \times (1.2 \times 10^7)$ .... (1 mark)
   c) $(1.2 \times 10^{-7}) \div (2 \times 10^{-4})$ .... (1 mark)
   d) $(8.9 \times 10^6) \div (4 \times 10^{-2})$ .... (1 mark)

4 The mass of an atom is 2×10^{-23} grams.
   What is the total mass of 9×10^{15} of these atoms? .... (3 marks)

Score   / 15

C These are GCSE style questions. Answer all parts of the questions. Show your workings (on separate paper if necessary) and include the correct units in your answers.

1 a) i) Write the number 2.07×10^5 as an ordinary number.

....

ii) Write the number 0.000 046 in standard form.

.... (2 marks)

b) Multiply 7×10^4 by 5×10^7

Give your answer in standard form.

.... (2 marks)

2 Calculate the value of $\dfrac{4.68 \times 10^9 + 3.14 \times 10^7}{2.14 \times 10^{-3}}$

Give your answer in standard form, correct to 2 significant figures.

.... (3 marks)

3 3.8×10^8 seeds weigh 1 kilogram.

Each seed weighs the same. Calculate the weight in grams of one seed.

Give your answer in standard form, correct to 2 significant figures.

.... g (2 marks)

4 If $a = 3.2 \times 10^4$ and $b = 2 \times 10^{-3}$, calculate the answer to $\dfrac{b^2}{a+b}$

giving your answer in standard form, correct to 3 significant figures.

.... (2 marks)

Score   / 11

How well did you do?
1–9 marks   Try again
10–19 marks Getting there
20–26 marks Good work
27–31 marks Excellent!

TOTAL SCORE   / 31

For more information on this topic see pages 24–25 of your Success Guide.

RECURRING DECIMALS AND SURDS

A Choose just one answer, a, b, c or d.

1. Which fraction is the same as $0.\dot{5}$?
   a) $\frac{1}{2}$
   b) $\frac{5}{10}$
   c) $\frac{5}{9}$
   d) $\frac{5}{8}$ (1 mark)

2. Which fraction is equivalent to 0.636363...?
   a) $\frac{63}{100}$
   b) $\frac{6}{99}$
   c) $\frac{636}{999}$
   d) $\frac{7}{11}$ (1 mark)

3. Which fraction is equivalent to 0.211111...?
   a) $\frac{19}{90}$
   b) $\frac{21}{99}$
   c) $\frac{211}{999}$
   d) $\frac{2}{9}$ (1 mark)

4. Which expression is equivalent to $\sqrt{12}$?
   a) $2\sqrt{6}$
   b) $2\sqrt{3}$
   c) $6\sqrt{2}$
   d) $3\sqrt{2}$ (1 mark)

5. Which expression is equivalent to $\frac{1}{\sqrt{3}}$?
   a) $\frac{\sqrt{3}}{3}$
   b) $\frac{\sqrt{3}}{9}$
   c) $\frac{9}{\sqrt{3}}$
   d) $\frac{3}{\sqrt{3}}$ (1 mark)

Score / 5

B Answer all parts of the questions.

1. Match each of the recurring decimals to the equivalent fraction.

   $0.\dot{3}$ $\frac{7}{9}$

   $0.\dot{7}$ $\frac{244}{333}$

   $0.\dot{2}\dot{4}$ $\frac{13}{30}$

   $0.\dot{7}3\dot{2}$ $\frac{1}{3}$

   $0.4\dot{3}$ $\frac{8}{33}$

   (5 marks)

2. Find the fraction which is equivalent to $0.12\dot{5}$. Express the fraction in its simplest form.

   ....

   .... (2 marks)

3. Express each of the following in the form $a\sqrt{b}$, where a and b are integers and b is as small as possible.
   a) $\sqrt{24}$ .... (1 mark)
   b) $\sqrt{75}$ .... (1 mark)
   c) $\sqrt{48} + \sqrt{12}$ .... (2 marks)
   d) $\sqrt{80} + \sqrt{20}$ .... (2 marks)

Score / 13

C These are GCSE style questions. Answer all parts of the questions. Show your workings (on separate paper if necessary) and include the correct units in your answers.

1 a) Change the decimal $0.5\dot{4}$ into a fraction in its lowest terms.
....
(2 marks)

b) Write the recurring decimal $0.02\dot{6}$ as a fraction.
....
(2 marks)

2 a) Find the value of $\sqrt{3} \times \sqrt{27}$ .... (1 mark)

b) $\sqrt{3} + \sqrt{27} = a\sqrt{3}$, where a is an integer.

Find the value of a.
....
(1 mark)

c) Find the value of $\dfrac{\sqrt{3} + \sqrt{12}}{\sqrt{75}}$

....
(3 marks)

3 Work out $\dfrac{(5 + \sqrt{5})(2 - 2\sqrt{5})}{\sqrt{45}}$

Give your answer in its simplest form.
....
(3 marks)

4 Write down the recurring decimal $0.1\dot{2}\dot{3}$ in the form $\dfrac{a}{b}$ where a and b are integers.
....
(2 marks)

5 Simplify $(4 - \sqrt{3})^2$
....
(2 marks)

6 Express $\dfrac{\sqrt{125} + \sqrt{50}}{\sqrt{5}}$ in the form $a + \sqrt{b}$

(4 marks)

7 Work out $\dfrac{(2 - \sqrt{2})(4 + 3\sqrt{2})}{2}$

Give your answer in the form $a + b\sqrt{c}$
....
(3 marks)

8 Write down the recurring decimal $0.\dot{7}\dot{5}$ as a fraction in its simplest form.
....
(2 marks)

Score   / 25

How well did you do?
1–13 marks   Try again
14–25 marks Getting there
26–36 marks Good work
37–43 marks Excellent!

TOTAL SCORE   / 43

For more information on this topic see page 27 of your Success Guide.

DIRECT AND INVERSE PROPORTION

A

Choose just one answer, a, b, c or d.

1 If a is directly proportional to b and $a = 10$ when $b = 5$, what is the formula that connects a and b?
 a) $a = 5b$
 b) $a = 10b$
 c) $a = \frac{1}{2}b$
 d) $a = 2b$ (1 mark)

2 If y is directly proportional to x and $y = 12$ when $x = 4$, what is the formula that connects x and y?
 a) $y = 3x$
 b) $x = 3y$
 c) $y = 12x$
 d) $y = \frac{1}{3x}$ (1 mark)

3 If d is inversely proportional to c, so that $d = \frac{k}{c}$ and $d = 6$ when $c = 3$, what is the value of k?
 a) 12   b) 18   c) 2   d) 9 (1 mark)

4 If v is inversely proportional to w^2 and $v = 3$ when $w = 2$, what is the formula that connects v and w^2?
 a) $v = \frac{18}{w^2}$
 b) $v = \frac{2}{w^2}$
 c) $v = \frac{12}{w^2}$
 d) $v = \frac{3}{2w^2}$ (1 mark)

Score   / 4

B

Answer all parts of the questions.

1 Given that $a \propto b$, calculate the values missing from this table.

a		12	30
b	2		6

(2 marks)

2 The variables x and y are related so that y is directly proportional to the square of x. Complete this table for values of x and y.

x	2	4		
y	12		27	75

(3 marks)

3 z is inversely proportional to the square of v.

a) Express z in terms of v and a constant of proportionality k.

.... (2 marks)

b) If z = 10 when v = 5, calculate

i) the value of z when v = 2 .... (2 marks)

ii) the value of v when z = 1000 .... (2 marks)

Score   / 11

C These are GCSE style questions. Answer all parts of the questions. Show your workings (on separate paper if necessary) and include the correct units in your answers.

1 The extension E of a spring is directly proportional to the force F pulling the spring. The extension is 6 cm when a force of 15 N is pulling it.

Calculate the extension when the force is 80 N.

....

.... (4 marks)

2 The volume (V) of a toy is proportional to the cube of its height (h). When the toy's volume is 60 cm³ the height is 2 cm. Find the volume of a similar toy whose height is 5 cm.

....

.... (4 marks)

3 I is inversely proportional to the square of d.

When d equals 2, I equals 50.

a) Calculate the value of I when d is 3.5.

....

.... (3 marks)

b) Calculate the value of d when I equals 12.5.

....

.... (3 marks)

4 c is inversely proportional to b and b = 10 when c = 4.

Daisy says that the formula connecting c and b is given by $c = \dfrac{40}{b}$.

Decide whether Daisy is correct, giving a reason for your answer.

....

.... (2 marks)

Score / 16

How well did you do?
1–6 marks Try again
7–13 marks Getting there
14–21 marks Good work
22–31 marks Excellent!

TOTAL SCORE / 31

For more information on this topic see page 26 of your Success Guide.

UPPER AND LOWER BOUNDS OF MEASUREMENT

A
Choose just one answer, a, b, c or d.

1 The length of an object is 5.6 cm, correct to the nearest millimetre. What is the lower bound of the length of the object?
a) 5.56 cm
b) 5.55 cm
c) 5.64 cm
d) 5.65 cm (1 mark)

2 The weight of an object is 2.23 grammes, correct to two decimal places. What is the upper bound of the weight of the object?
a) 2.225 g
b) 2.234 g
c) 2.235 g
d) 2.32 g (1 mark)

3 A hall can hold 40 people to the nearest ten. What is the upper boundary for the number of people in the hall?
a) 45
b) 35
c) 44
d) 36 (1 mark)

4 A square has a length of 3 cm to the nearest centimetre. What is the lower bound for the perimeter of the square?
a) 12 cm
b) 10 cm
c) 10.4 cm
d) 14 cm (1 mark)

5 Using the information given in the previous question, what is the upper bound for the area of the square?
a) 6.25 cm^2
b) 9 cm^2
c) 12.5 cm^2
d) 12.25 cm^2 (1 mark)

Score / 5

B
Answer all parts of the questions.

1 Complete the inequalities in the questions below, which show the upper and lower bounds of some measurements.

a) .... ≤ 5.24 < 5.245 (1 mark)

b) 3.5 ≤ 4 < .... (1 mark)

c) 0.3235 ≤ 0.324 < .... (1 mark)

d) 8.435 ≤ .... < 8.445 (1 mark)

2 $a = \dfrac{(3.4)^2 \times 12.68}{2.4}$

3.4 and 2.4 are correct to 1 decimal place.

12.68 is correct to 2 decimal places.

Which of the following calculations gives the lower bound for *a* and the upper bound for *a*? Write down the letters.

A $\dfrac{(3.45)^2 \times 12.685}{2.35}$

B $\dfrac{(3.35)^2 \times 12.675}{2.35}$

C $\dfrac{(3.45)^2 \times 12.685}{2.45}$

D $\dfrac{(3.45)^2 \times 12.675}{2.35}$

E $\dfrac{(3.35)^2 \times 12.675}{2.45}$

Lower bound .... Upper bound .... (2 marks)

Score / 6

C These are GCSE style questions. Answer all parts of the questions. Show your workings (on separate paper if necessary) and include the correct units in your answers.

1 p = 3.1 cm and q = 4.7 cm, correct to one decimal place.

   a) Calculate the upper bound for the value of p + q

   ....

   .... (2 marks)

   b) Calculate the lower bound for the value of $\frac{p}{q}$

   Give your answer correct to 3 significant figures.

   ....

   ....

   .... (3 marks)

2 The volume of a cube is given as 62.7 cm³, correct to 1 decimal place. Find the upper and lower bounds for the length of an edge of this cube.

   Lower bound = ...

   Upper bound = ... (4 marks)

3 The mass of an object is measured as 120 g, and its volume as 630 cm³. Both of these measurements are correct to 2 significant figures. Find the range of possible values for the density of the object.

   ....

   .... (4 marks)

4 To the nearest centimetre, a = 3 cm, b = 5 cm.

   Calculate the lower bound for ab. .... cm² (2 marks)

5 The weight of a bag of flour is 2 kg, but it is found to have a weight of 2.21 kg. Calculate the percentage error.

   ....

   .... (2 marks)

Score   / 17

How well did you do?
1–6 marks   Try again
7–11 marks   Getting there
12–18 marks Good work
19–28 marks Excellent!

TOTAL SCORE   / 28

For more information on this topic see pages 28–29 of your Success Guide.

UPPER AND LOWER BOUNDS OF MEASUREMENT

ALGEBRA

A
Choose just one answer, a, b, c or d.

1 What is the expression $7a - 4b + 6a - 3b$ when it is fully simplified?
   a) $7b - a$ b) $13a + 7b$
   c) $a - 7b$ d) $13a - 7b$ (1 mark)

2 If $m = \sqrt{\dfrac{r^2 p}{4}}$ and $r = 3$ and $p = 6$,
what is the value of m to 1 decimal place?
   a) 13.5   b) 182.3
   c) 3.7   d) 3   (1 mark)

3 What is $(n - 3)^2$ when it is multiplied out and simplified?
   a) $n^2 + 9$
   b) $n^2 + 6n - 9$
   c) $n^2 - 6n - 9$
   d) $n^2 - 6n + 9$ (1 mark)

4 $P = a^2 + b$. Rearrange this formula to make a the subject.
   a) $a = \pm\sqrt{(P - b)}$
   b) $a = \pm\sqrt{(P + b)}$
   c) $a = \dfrac{P - b}{2}$
   d) $a = \dfrac{P + b}{2}$ (1 mark)

5 Factorising $n^2 + 7n - 8$ gives:
   a) $(n - 2)(n - 6)$
   b) $(n - 2)(n + 4)$
   c) $(n - 1)(n + 8)$
   d) $(n + 1)(n - 8)$ (1 mark)

Score   / 5

B
Answer all parts of the questions.

1 John buys b books costing £6 each and p magazines costing 67 pence each. Write down a formula for the total cost (T) of the books and magazines.

   $T =$ ....   (2 marks)

2 $a = \dfrac{b^2 + 2c}{4}$

   a) Calculate a if $b = 2$ and $c = 6$. .... (1 mark)

   b) Calculate a if $b = 3$ and $c = 5.5$. .... (1 mark)

   c) Calculate b if $a = 25$ and $c = 18$. .... (1 mark)

3 Factorise the following expressions.

   a) $10n + 15$ .... (1 mark)   b) $24 - 36n$ .... (1 mark)

   c) $n^2 + 6n + 5$ .... (1 mark)   d) $n^2 - 64$ .... (1 mark)

   e) $n^2 - 3n - 4$ .... (1 mark)

4 Rearrange each of the formulas below to make b the subject.

   a) $p = 3b - 4$ .... (1 mark)

   b) $y = \dfrac{b^2 - 6}{4}$ .... (1 mark)

   c) $5(n + b) = 2b + 2$ .... (1 mark)

Score   / 13

C These are GCSE style questions. Answer all parts of the questions. Show your workings (on separate paper if necessary) and include the correct units in your answers.

1 Peter uses this formula to calculate the value of V.

$$V = \frac{\pi x(2R^2 + t^2)}{500}$$

$\pi = 3.14, \quad x = 20, \quad R = 5.2, \quad t = -4.1$

Calculate the value of V, giving your answer to 2 significant figures.

....

....

V = ... (3 marks)

2 a) Expand and simplify $3(2x + 1) - 2(x - 2)$

.... (2 marks)

b) (i) Factorise $6a + 12$

.... (1 mark)

(ii) Factorise completely $10a^2 - 15ab$

.... (2 marks)

c) (i) Factorise $n^2 + 5n + 6$

.... (2 marks)

(ii) Hence simplify fully $\dfrac{2(n + 3)}{n^2 + 5n + 6}$

.... (2 marks)

d) Factorise $(x + y)^2 - 2(x + y)$

.... (2 marks)

3 Show that $(n-1)^2 + n + (n-1)$ simplifies to n^2

....

....

.... (3 marks)

Score / 17

How well did you do?
1–13 marks Try again
14–18 marks Getting there
19–28 marks Good work
29–35 marks Excellent!

TOTAL SCORE   / 35

For more information on this topic see pages 32–35 of your Success Guide.

EQUATIONS

A Choose just one answer, a, b, c or d.

1. Solve the equation $4n - 2 = 10$
   a) $n = 4$
   b) $n = 2$
   c) $n = 3$
   d) $n = 3.5$ (1 mark)

2. Solve the equation $4(x + 3) = 16$
   a) $x = 9$
   b) $x = 7$
   c) $x = 4$
   d) $x = 1$ (1 mark)

3. Solve the equation $4(n + 2) = 8(n - 3)$
   a) $n = 16$
   b) $n = 8$
   c) $n = 4$
   d) $n = 12$ (1 mark)

4. Solve the equation $10 - 6n = 4n - 5$
   a) $n = 2$
   b) $n = -2$
   c) $n = 1.5$
   d) $n = -1.5$ (1 mark)

5. What is the value of k in $y^k = y^{\frac{1}{2}} \div \frac{1}{\sqrt{y}}$
   a) 2
   b) $\frac{1}{2}$
   c) 1
   d) -2 (1 mark)

Score / 5

B Answer all parts of the questions.

1. Solve the following equations.
   a) $5n = 25$ ....
   b) $\frac{n}{3} = 12$ ....
   c) $2n - 4 = 10$ ....
   d) $3 - 2n = 14$ ....
   e) $\frac{n}{5} + 2 = 7$ ....
   f) $4 - \frac{n}{2} = 2$ .... (6 marks)

2. Solve the following equations.
   a) $12n + 5 = 3n + 32$ ....
   b) $5n - 4 = 3n + 6$ ....
   c) $5(n + 1) = 25$ ....
   d) $4(n - 2) = 3(n + 2)$ .... (4 marks)

3. Solve the following equations.
   a) $n^2 - 4n = 0$ ....
   b) $n^2 + 6n + 5 = 0$ ....
   c) $n^2 - 5n + 6 = 0$ ....
   d) $n^2 - 3n - 28 = 0$ .... (4 marks)

4. The angles in a triangle add up to 180°. Form an equation in n and solve it.

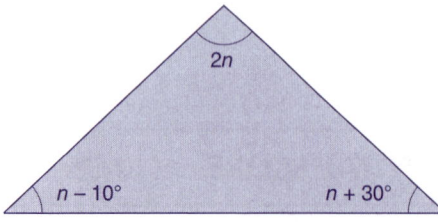

$n = $ .... (2 marks)

Score / 16

C These are GCSE style questions. Answer all parts of the questions. Show your workings (on separate paper if necessary) and include the correct units in your answers.

1 Solve these equations.

a) $5m - 3 = 12$

m = ... (2 marks)

b) $8p + 3 = 9 - 2p$

p = ... (2 marks)

c) $5(x - 1) = 3x + 7$

x = ... (2 marks)

d) $\dfrac{w}{2} + \dfrac{(3w + 2)}{3} = \dfrac{1}{3}$

w = ... (2 marks)

2 a) Factorise $x^2 - 4x + 3$

.... (2 marks)

b) Hence solve the equation $x^2 - 4x + 3 = 0$

x = ...

and x = ... (1 mark)

3 The area of the rectangle is 125 cm². Work out the value of k.

k = ... (3 marks)

4 Solve the following equations

(i) $3^{2k + 1} = 27$

.... (1 mark)

(ii) $16^{k-3} = 64$

.... (2 marks)

Score / 17

How well did you do?
1–10 marks Try again
11–21 marks Getting there
22–27 marks Good work
28–38 marks Excellent!

TOTAL SCORE   / 38

For more information on this topic see pages 36–37 of your Success Guide.

EQUATIONS AND INEQUALITIES

A

Choose just one answer, a, b, c or d.

1 Solve these simultaneous equations to find the values of *a* and *b*.
$a + b = 10$
$2a - b = 2$
a) $a = 4, b = 6$
b) $a = 4, b = -2$
c) $a = 5, b = 5$
d) $a = 3, b = 7$ (1 mark)

2 Solve these simultaneous equations to find the values of *x* and *y*.
$3x - y = 7$
$2x + y = 3$
a) $x = 3, y = 2$
b) $x = 2, y = 1$
c) $x = -3, y = 2$
d) $x = 2, y = -1$ (1 mark)

3 The equation $y^3 + 2y = 82$ has a solution between 4 and 5. By using a method of trial and improvement, find the solution to 1 decimal place.
a) 3.9   b) 4.1   c) 4.2   d) 4.3 (1 mark)

4 Solve the inequality $3x + 1 < 19$
a) $x < 3$ b) $x < 7$
c) $x < 5$ d) $x < 6$ (1 mark)

5 Solve the inequality $2x - 7 < 9$
a) $x < 9$ b) $x < 10$
c) $x < 8$ d) $x < 6.5$ (1 mark)

Score / 5

B

Answer all parts of the questions.

1 Solve these simultaneous equations to find the values of *a* and *b*.

a) $2a + b = 8$
$3a - b = 2$

a = ...
b = ... (2 marks)

b) $5a + b = 24$
$2a + 2b = 24$

a = ...
b = ... (2 marks)

c) $a - b = 7$
$3a + 2b = 11$

a = ...
b = ... (2 marks)

d) $4a + 3b = 6$
$2a - 3b = 12$

a = ...
b = ... (2 marks)

2 Use a trial and improvement method to solve the following equation. Give your answer to 1 decimal place.

$t^2 - 2t = 20$ t = ... (2 marks)

3 Solve the following inequalities.

a) $5x + 2 < 12$

.... (1 mark)

b) $\frac{x}{3} + 1 \geq 3$

.... (1 mark)

c) $3 \leq 2x + 1 \leq 9$

.... (1 mark)

d) $3 \leq 3x + 2 \leq 8$

.... (1 mark)

Score / 14

C These are GCSE style questions. Answer all parts of the questions. Show your workings (on separate paper if necessary) and include the correct units in your answers.

1 *n* is an integer.

   a) Write down the values of n which satisfy the inequality $-4 < n \leq 2$

   .... (2 marks)

   b) Solve the inequality $5p - 2 \leq 8$

   .... (2 marks)

2 Use the method of trial and improvement to solve the equation $x^3 + 3x = 28$

Give your answer correct to one decimal place.

You must show **all** your working.

....

....

....

   $x = $ .... (4 marks)

3 Solve these simultaneous equations.

   $3x - 2y = -12$

   $2x + 6y = 3$

   $x = $ ....

   $y = $ .... (4 marks)

4 Solve these simultaneous equations.

   a) $2a - b = 14$

   $a + 3b = 14$

   $a = $ ....

   $b = $ .... (2 marks)

   b) $5a + 4b = 23$

   $3a - 5b = -1$

   $a = $ ....

   $b = $ .... (2 marks)

Score   / 16

How well did you do?

1–9 marks   Try again
10–19 marks   Getting there
20–27 marks   Good work
28–35 marks   Excellent!

TOTAL SCORE   / 35

For more information on this topic see pages 38–39 and 42 of your Success Guide.

FURTHER ALGEBRA AND EQUATIONS

A
Choose just one answer, a, b, c or d.

1. The quadratic equation $x^2 + 4x + 7$ is written in the form $(x + a)^2 + b$. What are the values of a and b?
   a) $a = 3, b = 6$
   b) $a = 4, b = -3$
   c) $a = 2, b = 3$
   d) $a = 4, b = 2$

   (1 mark)

2. What are the solutions of the quadratic equation $2x^2 + 5x + 2 = 0$?
   a) $x = -\frac{1}{2}, x = -2$
   b) $x = \frac{1}{2}, x = -2$
   c) $x = -\frac{1}{2}, x = 2$
   d) $x = 2, x = -2$

   (1 mark)

3. What are the solutions of the quadratic equation $x^2 - 4 = 0$?
   a) $x = 2, x = 2$
   b) $x = -2, x = -2$
   c) $x = 0, x = 4$
   d) $x = 2, x = -2$

   (1 mark)

4. What are the solutions of the quadratic equation $6x^2 + 2x = 8$?
   a) $x = 1, x = \frac{3}{4}$
   b) $x = 1, x = -\frac{4}{3}$
   c) $x = -1, x = \frac{4}{3}$
   d) $x = -1, x = -\frac{3}{4}$

   (1 mark)

5. The quadratic equation $x^2 - 2x + 3$ is written in the form $(x + a)^2 + b$. What are the values of a and b?
   a) $a = 1, b = 2$
   b) $a = -1, b = -2$
   c) $a = -1, b = 2$
   d) $a = 1, b = -2$

   (1 mark)

Score   / 5

B
Answer all parts of the questions.

1. a) Factorise $x^2 + 11x + 30$ .... (2 marks)

   b) Write the following as a single fraction in its simplest form:

   $$\frac{4}{x + 6} + \frac{4}{x^2 + 11x + 30}$$ ....

   (4 marks)

2. $(x + 4)(x - 3) = 2$

   a) Show that $x^2 + x - 14 = 0$

   .... (2 marks)

   b) Solve the equation $x^2 + x - 14 = 0$

   Give your answers correct to 3 significant figures.

   .... (3 marks)

3. The formula $a = \frac{3(b + c)}{bc}$ is rearranged to make c the subject. Greg says the answer is $c = \frac{3b}{ab - 3}$

   Decide whether Greg is right. You must justify your answer.

   ....
   .... (3 marks)

Score   / 14

C These are GCSE style questions. Answer all parts of the questions. Show your workings (on separate paper if necessary) and include the correct units in your answers.

1 The diagram shows a right-angled triangle with base $(x - 3)$ and height $(x + 4)$.
All measurements are given in centimetres.

The area of the triangle is 12 square centimetres.

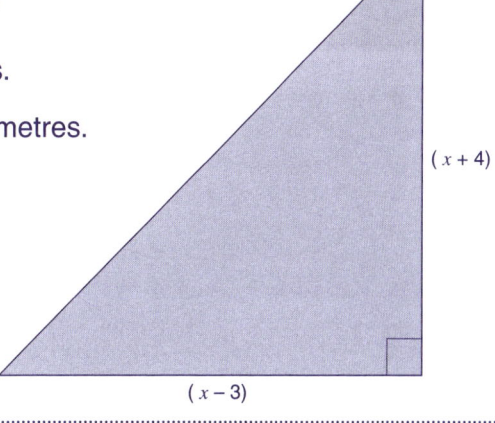

$(x + 4)$

$(x - 3)$

a) Show that $x^2 + x - 36 = 0$

....

.... (3 marks)

b) Find the base of the triangle. Give your answer correct to 2 decimal places.

....

....

.... cm (4 marks)

2 Make b the subject of the formula $a = \dfrac{8b + 5}{4 - 3b}$

....

.... (4 marks)

3 The expression $x^2 + 6x + 3$ can be written in the form $(x + a)^2 + b$ for all values of x.

a) Find a and b.

$a = $ ....

$b = $ .... (3 marks)

b) The expression $x^2 + 6x + 3$ has a minimum value. Find this minimum value.

....

.... (1 mark)

Score   / 15

How well did you do?
1–7 marks Try again
8–16 marks Getting there
17–25 marks Good work
26–34 marks Excellent!

TOTAL SCORE   / 34

For more information on this topic see pages 40–41 of your Success Guide.

STRAIGHT LINE GRAPHS

A

Choose just one answer, a, b, c or d.

1. Which pair of coordinates lies on the line $x = 2$?
   a) (1, 3)
   b) (2, 3)
   c) (3, 2)
   d) (0, 2) (1 mark)

2. Which pair of coordinates lies on the line $y = -3$?
   a) (−3, 5)
   b) (5, −2)
   c) (−2, 5)
   d) (5, −3) (1 mark)

3. What is the gradient of the line $y = 2 - 5x$?
   a) −2
   b) −5
   c) 2
   d) 5 (1 mark)

4. These graphs have been drawn: $y = 3x - 1$, $y = 5 - 2x$, $y = 6x + 1$, $y = 2x - 3$
   Which graph is the steepest?
   a) $y = 3x - 1$
   b) $y = 5 - 2x$
   c) $y = 6x + 1$
   d) $y = 2x - 3$ (1 mark)

5. At what point does the graph $y = 3x - 4$ intercept the y axis?
   a) (0, −4)
   b) (0, 3)
   c) (−4, 0)
   d) (3, 0) (1 mark)

Score / 5

B

Answer all parts of the questions.

1. a) On the grid, draw the graph of $y = 6 - x$
   Join your points with a straight line.

   (2 marks)

   b) A second line goes through the coordinates (1, 5), (−2, −4) and (2, 8)

   i) Draw this line. (1 mark)

   ii) Write down the equation of the line you have just drawn.

   .... (2 marks)

   c) What are the coordinates of the point where the two lines meet?

   .... (1 mark)

2. The equations of five straight lines are: $y = 2x - 4$, $y = 3 - 2x$, $y = 4 - 2x$, $y = 5x - 4$, $y = 3x - 5$
   Two of the lines are parallel.
   Write down the equations of these two lines. .... and .... (2 marks)

Score / 8

C This is a GCSE style question. Answer all parts of the question. Show your workings (on separate paper if necessary) and include the correct units in your answers.

1 The line with equation $3y + 2x = 12$ has been drawn on the grid.

$3y + 2x = 12$

a) Write down the gradient of the line $3y + 2x = 12$

.... (2 marks)

b) Write down the equation of the line which is parallel to $3y + 2x = 12$ and passes through the point with coordinates (0, 2)

.... (1 mark)

c) On the grid above draw the graph with the equation $3y - x = 3$ (2 marks)

d) Write down the coordinates of the point of intersection of the two straight-line graphs.

(............, ...) (1 mark)

e) Write down the gradient of a line which is perpendicular to the line $3y + 2x = 12$

.... (1 mark)

Score   / 7

How well did you do?
1–4 marks   Try again
5–9 marks   Getting there
10–14 marks Good work
15–20 marks Excellent!

TOTAL SCORE   / 20

For more information on this topic see pages 44–45 of your Success Guide.

CURVED GRAPHS

A Choose just one answer, a, b, c or d.

1. Which pair of coordinates lies on the graph $y = x^2 - 2$?
   a) (1, 1)
   b) (4, 14)
   c) (2, 4)
   d) (0, 2) (1 mark)

2. On which of these curves do the coordinates (2, 5) lie?
   a) $y = x^2 - 4$
   b) $y = 2x^2 + 3$
   c) $y = x^2 - 6$
   d) $y = 2x^2 - 3$ (1 mark)

Questions 3–5 refer to the diagrams above.

3. What is the equation of curve A?
   a) $y = 5 - 2x^2$ b) $y = x^2 + 4x + 4$
   c) $y = x^3 + 2$ d) $y = 4 - x^2$ (1 mark)

4. What is the equation of curve B?
   a) $y = 5 - 2x^2$ b) $y = x^2 + 4x + 4$
   c) $y = x^3 + 2$ d) $y = 4 - x^2$ (1 mark)

5. What is the equation of curve C?
   a) $y = 5 - 2x^2$ b) $y = x^2 + 4x + 4$
   c) $y = x^3 + 2$ d) $y = 4 - x^2$ (1 mark)

Score / 5

B Answer all parts of the questions.

1. a) Complete the table of values for $y = x^2 - 2x - 2$

x	-2	-1	0	1	2	3
$y = x^2 - 2x - 2$		-2			1	

(2 marks)

   b) On the grid below draw the graph of $y = x^2 - 2x - 2$ (3 marks)

   c) Use your graph to write down an estimate for:

   i) the minimum value of y.

   y = ... (1 mark)

   ii) the solutions of the equation $x^2 - 2x - 2 = 0$

   x = ... and x = ... (2 marks)

Score / 8

C This is a GCSE style question. Answer all parts of the question. Show your workings (on separate paper if necessary) and include the correct units in your answers.

1 The line with equation $3y + 2x = 12$ has been drawn on the grid.

a) Write down the gradient of the line $3y + 2x = 12$

.... (2 marks)

b) Write down the equation of the line which is parallel to $3y + 2x = 12$ and passes through the point with coordinates (0, 2)

.... (1 mark)

c) On the grid above draw the graph with the equation $3y - x = 3$ (2 marks)

d) Write down the coordinates of the point of intersection of the two straight-line graphs.

(............, ...) (1 mark)

e) Write down the gradient of a line which is perpendicular to the line $3y + 2x = 12$

.... (1 mark)

Score / 7

How well did you do?
1–4 marks   Try again
5–9 marks   Getting there
10–14 marks Good work
15–20 marks Excellent!

TOTAL SCORE   / 20

For more information on this topic see pages 44–45 of your Success Guide.

CURVED GRAPHS

A Choose just one answer, a, b, c or d.

1. Which pair of coordinates lies on the graph $y = x^2 - 2$?
   a) (1, 1)
   b) (4, 14)
   c) (2, 4)
   d) (0, 2) (1 mark)

2. On which of these curves do the coordinates (2, 5) lie?
   a) $y = x^2 - 4$
   b) $y = 2x^2 + 3$
   c) $y = x^2 - 6$
   d) $y = 2x^2 - 3$ (1 mark)

Questions 3–5 refer to the diagrams above.

3. What is the equation of curve A?
   a) $y = 5 - 2x^2$ b) $y = x^2 + 4x + 4$
   c) $y = x^3 + 2$ d) $y = 4 - x^2$ (1 mark)

4. What is the equation of curve B?
   a) $y = 5 - 2x^2$ b) $y = x^2 + 4x + 4$
   c) $y = x^3 + 2$ d) $y = 4 - x^2$ (1 mark)

5. What is the equation of curve C?
   a) $y = 5 - 2x^2$ b) $y = x^2 + 4x + 4$
   c) $y = x^3 + 2$ d) $y = 4 - x^2$ (1 mark)

Score / 5

B Answer all parts of the questions.

1. a) Complete the table of values for $y = x^2 - 2x - 2$

x	-2	-1	0	1	2	3
$y = x^2 - 2x - 2$		-2			1	

(2 marks)

b) On the grid below draw the graph of $y = x^2 - 2x - 2$ (3 marks)

c) Use your graph to write down an estimate for:

i) the minimum value of y.

y = ... (1 mark)

ii) the solutions of the equation $x^2 - 2x - 2 = 0$

x = ... and x = ... (2 marks)

Score / 8

C This is a GCSE style question. Answer all parts of the question. Show your workings (on separate paper if necessary) and include the correct units in your answers.

1 a) Complete the table of values for the graph of $y = x^3 - 4$

x	-2	-1	0	1	2	3
$y = x^3 - 4$		-5				23

(2 marks)

b) On the grid, draw the graph of $y = x^3 - 4$

(2 marks)

c) Use your graph to find an estimate of:

i) the solution of the equation $x^3 - 4 = 0$

$x = $ .... (1 mark)

ii) the solution of the equation $x^3 - 4 = 10$

$x = $ .... (2 marks)

iii) the solution of the equation $x^3 - 4 = 2$

$x = $ .... (2 marks)

iv) the solution of the equation $x^3 - 4 = -7$

$x = $ .... (2 marks)

Score / 11

How well did you do?
1–4 correct   Try again
5–9 correct   Getting there
10–16 correct Good work
17–24 correct Excellent!

TOTAL SCORE   / 24

For more on this topic see pages 46–47 of your Success Guide.

HARDER WORK ON GRAPHS

A

Choose just one answer, a, b, c or d.

1. Solve these simultaneous equations to find values for *a* and *b*.
   $a^2 + b^2 = 13$
   $2a + b = 7$
   a) $a = -2, b = 3$
   b) $a = 3, b = 2$
   c) $a = 2, b = 3$
   d) $a = 2, b = -3$ (1 mark)

2. Solve these simultaneous equations to find values for *a* and *b*.
   $a^2 - b = 3$
   $3a + b = 1$
   a) $a = 1, b = -2$
   b) $a = -1, b = 2$
   c) $a = -1, b = -2$
   d) $a = 1, b = 2$ (1 mark)

3. What are the coordinates of a point where the line $y = 4 - x$ and the circle $x^2 + y^2 = 40$ meet?
   a) $x = 2, y = -6$
   b) $x = 2, y = 6$
   c) $x = -2, y = -6$
   d) $x = -2, y = 6$ (1 mark)

4. The graph $y = x^2$ is translated 2 units to the left. What is the equation of the new curve?
   a) $y = (x - 2)^2$
   b) $y = x^2 + 2$
   c) $y = (x + 2)^2$
   d) $y = x^2 - 2$ (1 mark)

Score / 4

B

Answer all parts of the questions.

1. This is a sketch of the curve with equation $y = f(x)$

   The maximum point of the curve is A (2, 7)

   Write down the coordinates of the maximum point for each of the following curves.

   a) $y = f(x) - 3$ (............, ...)
   b) $y = f(x + 1)$ (............, ...)
   c) $y = f(x - 4)$ (............, ...)
   d) $y = f(-x)$ (............, ...)
   e) $y = f(2x)$ (............, ...) (5 marks)

2. Decide whether this statement is true or false.

   'The line with the equation $2x - y = 6$ intersects with the circle $x^2 + y^2 = 17$ at the point $(1, -4)$'
   Explain your reasoning.

   ....

   .... (2 marks)

   Score / 7

C These are GCSE style questions. Answer all parts of the questions. Show your workings (on separate paper if necessary) and include the correct units in your answers.

1 a) Solve these simultaneous equations.

$x + 3y = -12$

$x^2 + y^2 = 34$

....

.... (5 marks)

b) Give a geometrical interpretation of the result.

....

.... (2 marks)

2 The graph of $y = f(x)$ is sketched in the diagrams below.

a)

Sketch the graph of $y = f(-x)$ on this grid. (2 marks)

b)

Sketch the graph of $y = f(x + 2)$ on this grid. (2 marks)

Score   / 11

How well did you do?

1–4 marks   Try again
5–8 marks   Getting there
9–15 marks Good work
16–22 marks Excellent!

TOTAL SCORE   / 22

For more information on this topic see pages 48–49 of your Success Guide.

INTERPRETING GRAPHS

A Choose just one answer, a, b, c or d.

Use the graph opposite for these questions.
The graph shows Mrs Morgan's car journey.

1. At what speed did Mrs Morgan travel for the first hour and a half?
   a) 25 mph
   b) 28 mph
   c) 30 mph
   d) 26.7 mph   (1 mark)

2. At what time did Mrs Morgan take a break from her car journey?
   a) 1530
   b) 1600
   c) 1400
   d) 1500   (1 mark)

3. At what speed did Mrs Morgan travel between 1700 and 1800 hours?
   a) 60 mph
   b) 80 mph
   c) 35 mph
   d) 40 mph   (1 mark)

Score / 3

B Answer all parts of the questions.

1. Water is poured into these odd-shaped vases at a constant rate. Match each vase to the correct graph.

   Vase A matches graph ....
   Vase B matches graph ....
   Vase C matches graph ....   (3 marks)

2. This is the graph of $y = x^2 - x - 6$

   a) Use the graph to find the roots of the equation
   $x^2 - x - 6 = 0$
   .... and ....   (2 marks)

   b) By drawing suitable straight lines on the graph solve these equations:

   i) $x^2 - x - 6 = 2$ ....   (2 marks)

   ii) $x^2 - 7 = 0$ ....   (3 marks)

Score / 10

C These are GCSE style questions. Answer all parts of the questions. Show your workings (on separate paper if necessary) and include the correct units in your answers.

1 In an experiment, these values of the variables R and T were obtained.

R	0	1	2	3	4
T	5	8	17	32	53

The variables R and T are thought to satisfy a relationship of the form

$T = aR^2 + b$

a) On the axes draw a graph to test this.

(4 marks)

b) Use your graph to estimate the values of a and b.

a = ...

b = ... (2 marks)

c) Use your relationship to find T when R = 12

T = ... (1 mark)

2 The sketch graph shows a curve $y = ab^x$ where $b > 0$

(3,54)

Diagram not drawn to scale

(1,6)

The curve passes through the points (1, 6) and (3, 54)

Calculate the values of a and b.

a = ...

b = ... (3 marks)

Score / 10

How well did you do?
1–4 marks Try again
5–9 marks Getting there
10–16 marks Good work
17–23 marks Excellent!

TOTAL SCORE / 23

For more information on this topic see pages 50–51 of your Success Guide.

BEARINGS AND SCALE DRAWINGS

A Choose just one answer, a, b, c or d.

1. The bearing of P from Q is 050°. What is the bearing of Q from P?
   a) 130°
   b) 50°
   c) 230°
   d) 310° (1 mark)

2. The bearing of R from S is 130°. What is the bearing of S from R?
   a) 310°
   b) 230°
   c) 050°
   d) 200° (1 mark)

3. The bearing of A from B is 240°. What is the bearing of B from A?
   a) 120°
   b) 60°
   c) 320°
   d) 060° (1 mark)

4. The length of a car park is 25 metres. A scale diagram of the car park is being drawn to a scale of 1 cm to 5 metres. What is the length of the car park on the scale diagram?
   a) 500 mm
   b) 5 cm
   c) 50 cm
   d) 5 m (1 mark)

Score / 4

B Answer all parts of the questions.

1. The scale on a road map is 1 : 50 000. Two towns are 20 cm apart on the map. Work out the real distance, in km, between them.

   .... km (2 marks)

2. A ship sails on a bearing of 065° for 10 km. It then continues on a bearing of 120° for a further 15 km to a port (P).

   a) On a separate piece of paper, draw, using a scale of 1 cm to 2 km, an accurate scale drawing of this information.

   (3 marks)

   b) Measure on your diagram the direct distance between the start and the port (P).

   .... km (1 mark)

   c) What is the bearing of port P from the starting point?

   ....° (1 mark)

3. Is this statement is true or false?

   'The bearing of B from A is 060°'

   .... (1 mark)

Score / 8

C These are GCSE style questions. Answer all parts of the questions. Show your workings (on separate paper if necessary) and include the correct units in your answers.

1

Scale: 1 cm represents 50 m

N
↑
A
• B
• C
• D

The scale drawing shows the positions of points A, B, C and D. Point C is due east of point A.

a) Use measurements from the drawing to find:

   i) the distance, in metres, of B from A. .... m (1 mark)

   ii) the bearing of B from A. .... ° (2 marks)

   iii) the bearing of D from B. .... ° (2 marks)

b) Point E is 250 m from C on a bearing of 055°. Mark the position of point E on the diagram above. (2 marks)

2 Here is a sketch of a triangle.

Use a scale of 1 cm to 2 m to make an accurate scale drawing of the triangle.

Diagram not drawn to scale

9 m   12 m

14 m

(3 marks)

Score / 10

How well did you do?
1–4 marks   Try again
5–10 marks Getting there
11–16 marks Good work
17–22 marks Excellent!

TOTAL SCORE   / 22

For more information on this topic see pages 58–59 of your Success Guide.

45

TRANSFORMATIONS 1

A Choose just one answer, a, b, c or d.
Questions 1–4 refer to the diagram opposite.

1. What is the transformation that would map shape A onto shape B?
   a) reflection   b) rotation
   c) translation   d) enlargement   (1 mark)

2. What is the transformation that would map shape A onto shape C?
   a) reflection   b) rotation
   c) translation   d) enlargement   (1 mark)

3. What is the transformation that would map shape A onto shape D?
   a) reflection   b) rotation
   c) translation   d) enlargement   (1 mark)

4. What special name is given to triangles A, B, C, and D?
   a) enlargement   b) congruent
   c) translation   d) similar   (1 mark)

Score / 4

B Answer all parts of the questions.

1. On the grid carry out the following transformations.

   a) Reflect shape A in the y axis. Call the shape R.

   b) Rotate shape A 90° clockwise, about (0, 0). Call the shape S.

   c) Translate shape A by the vector $\begin{pmatrix} -3 \\ 4 \end{pmatrix}$. Call the shape T.

   (3 marks)

2. All the following shapes are either a reflection, rotation or translation of object P. State the transformation that has taken place for each of the following.

   a) P is transformed to A ....
   b) P is transformed to B ....
   c) P is transformed to C ....
   d) P is transformed to D ....

   (4 marks)

Score / 7

C These are GCSE style questions. Answer all parts of the questions. Show your workings (on separate paper if necessary) and include the correct units in your answers.

1

a) Describe fully the single transformation which takes shape A onto shape B.

....

.... (2 marks)

b) Describe fully the single transformation which takes shape A onto shape C.

....

.... (3 marks)

2

The triangle R has been drawn on the grid.

a) Rotate triangle R 90° clockwise about the point T (0, 1) and call the image P. (3 marks)

b) Translate triangle R by the vector $\begin{pmatrix} -4 \\ -3 \end{pmatrix}$ and call the image Q. (3 marks)

Score / 11

How well did you do?
1–6 marks   Try again
7–10 marks Getting there
11–16 marks Good work
17–22 marks Excellent!

TOTAL SCORE   / 22

For more information on this topic see pages 60–61 of your Success Guide.

TRANSFORMATIONS 2

A

Choose just one answer, a, b, c or d.

Questions 1–3 refer to the diagram drawn below.

1. Shape P is enlarged to give shape Q. What is the scale factor of the enlargement?
   a) $\frac{1}{3}$ b) 2
   c) 3   d) $\frac{1}{2}$ (1 mark)

2. Shape Q is enlarged to give shape P. What is the scale factor of the enlargement?
   a) $\frac{1}{3}$ b) 2
   c) 3   d) $\frac{1}{2}$ (1 mark)

3. What are the coordinates of the centre of enlargement?
   a) $(3, -2)$ b) $(-2, 3)$
   c) $(-3, 4)$ d) $(0, 0)$ (1 mark)

Score   / 3

B

Answer all parts of the questions.

1. The diagram shows the position of three shapes A, B and C.

   a) Describe the transformation which moves A onto C.
   .... (2 marks)

   b) Describe the transformation which moves A onto B.
   .... (2 marks)

   c) Describe the transformation which moves B onto C.
   .... (2 marks)

2. On the grid enlarge triangle PQR by a scale factor of −2, centre of enlargement at (0, 0) and call the enlarged shape P'Q'R'.

(3 marks)

Score   / 9

48

Letts

GCSE SUCCESS

VISUAL REVISION GUIDE

QUESTIONS & ANSWERS

BRAND NEW

HIGHER GCSE MATHS

Fiona C Mapp

ANSWER BOOK

ANSWERS

NUMBER

FRACTIONS

A
1. c
2. a
3. b
4. c
5. a

B
1. a) $\frac{5}{9}$
   b) $\frac{17}{44}$
   c) $\frac{3}{14}$
   d) 3
   e) $\frac{2}{3}$
   f) $\frac{5}{9}$
   g) $\frac{7}{8}$
   h) $2\frac{34}{49}$
2. a) $\frac{1}{7}$ $\frac{3}{10}$ $\frac{1}{2}$ $\frac{2}{3}$ $\frac{3}{4}$ $\frac{4}{5}$
   b) $\frac{1}{9}$ $\frac{2}{7}$ $\frac{1}{3}$ $\frac{2}{5}$ $\frac{5}{8}$ $\frac{3}{4}$
3. a) true
   b) false
4. 28 students

C
1. Jonathan, since $\frac{2}{3}$ is greater than $\frac{3}{5}$.
2. a) $1\frac{7}{15}$
   b) $\frac{16}{33}$
   c) $\frac{8}{63}$
   d) $\frac{3}{4}$
3. $\frac{7}{15}$

PERCENTAGES 1

A
1. c
2. c
3. a
4. d
5. b

B
1. a) £12
   b) £45
   c) £4
   d) 5 g
2. £26 265
3. 39%
4. 77%
5. £20
6. £225
7. 40%

C
1. a) £30.63
   b) £339.15
2. 20%
3. £70

PERCENTAGES 2

A
1. d
2. a
3. c
4. b

B
1. £168.03
2. £75.60
3. £6 969.60
4. £515.88
5. £135 475.20
6. 80.2 pence

C
1. a) £1000   b) £160
2. £1 337.11
3. a) 3.5%
   b) £757.12

FRACTIONS, DECIMALS AND PERCENTAGES

A
1. c
2. b
3. d
4. d
5. a

B
1.

Fraction	Decimal	Percentage
$\frac{2}{5}$	0.4	40%
$\frac{1}{20}$	0.05	5%
$\frac{1}{3}$	0.3	33.3%
$\frac{1}{25}$	0.04	4%
$\frac{1}{4}$	0.25	25%
$\frac{1}{8}$	0.125	12.5%

2. 30% $\frac{1}{3}$ 0.37 $\frac{3}{8}$ $\frac{1}{2}$ 0.62 92%
3. Both will give the same answer because increasing by 20% is the same as multiplying by 1.2. Finding 10% then doubling it gives 20%, which when you add it to 40, is the same as increasing £40 by 20%.

C
1. $\frac{1}{8}$ 25% 0.27 $\frac{1}{3}$ $\frac{2}{5}$ 0.571 72%
2. a) Ed's Electricals   : £225
      Sheila's Bargains : £217.38
      Gita's TV shop   : £232
      Maximum price = £232
      Minimum price = £217.38
   b) £200
3. 'Rosebushes' is cheaper because $\frac{1}{4}$ = 25% which is greater than the offer at 'Gardens are Us'.

APPROXIMATIONS AND USING A CALCULATOR

A
1. b
2. d
3. c
4. c
5. d

B
1. a) true
   b) false
   c) false
   d) true
2. a) 100
   b) 90
3. a) 365 (3 s.f.)
   b) 10.2 (3 s.f.)
   c) 6320 (3 s.f.)
   d) 0.0812 (3 s.f.)

C
1. a) 30 and 80
   b) 2400
   c) 49
2. 7.09 (3s.f.)
3. 5.937 102 5
   b) $\frac{30 \times 6}{40 - 10} = \frac{180}{30} = 6$
4. a) B
   b) B
   c) B
   d) A

RATIO

A
1. c
2. d
3. c
4. d
5. b

B
1. a) 1 : 1.5
   b) 1 : 1.6̇
   c) 1 : 3
2. 1200 ml
3. a) £10.25
   b) 48 g
4. £25 000
5. 4.5 days

C
1. Vicky £6 400
   Tracey £8 000
2. butter 75 g
   sugar   60 g
   eggs   3
   flour   67.5 g
   milk   22.5 ml
3. 6 days

INDICES

A
1. a
2. c
3. d
4. a
5. b

B
1. a) false
   b) false
   c) true
   d) true
   e) false
   f) true
2. a) 1
   b) $16a^8$
   c) $\frac{3}{4}a^{-3}$
   d) $27a^6b^9$
3. a) $4x^{-2}$
   b) a^2b^{-3}
   c) $3y^{-5}$
4. a) $\pm\frac{1}{5}$
   b) 343
   c) $\frac{25}{16}$
   d) $\frac{1}{27}$

C
1. a) p^7
   b) n^{-4} or $\frac{1}{n^4}$
   c) a^6
   d) $4ab$
2. a) 1
   b) $\frac{1}{25}$
   c) 648
   d) 16
   e) $\frac{1}{5}$
3. a) i) 1
      ii) $\frac{1}{16}$
      iii) $\pm\frac{3}{2} = \pm 1\frac{1}{2}$
   b) 5^4
4. a) $\frac{1}{125}$
   b) $\frac{9}{4}$
   c) $\frac{1}{4}$
5. a) 2^{-1}
   b) 2^{20}
   c) $2^{\frac{5}{2}}$
6. a) $\frac{1}{125x^3}$ b) $\frac{1}{16x^8y^{12}}$ c) $\frac{1}{27y^3}$

STANDARD INDEX FORM

A
1. b
2. b
3. a
4. b
5. b

B
1. a) true
   b) false
   c) false
   d) false
2. a) 8×10^{15}
   b) 1.4×10^4
   c) 3×10^{16}
   d) 8×10^3
3. a) 8.19×10^3
   b) 7.56×10^3
   c) 6×10^{-4}
   d) 2.225×10^8
4. 1.8×10^{-7} grams

C
1. a) i) 207 000
      ii) 4.6×10^{-5}
   b) 3.5×10^{12}
2. 2.2×10^{12}
3. 2.6×10^{-6}
4. 1.25×10^{-10}

RECURRING DECIMALS AND SURDS

A
1. c
2. d
3. a
4. b
5. a

B
1. $0.\dot{3} \rightarrow \frac{1}{3}$
   $0.\dot{7} \rightarrow \frac{7}{9}$
   $0.\dot{2}\dot{4} \rightarrow \frac{8}{33}$
   $0.7\dot{3}\dot{2} \rightarrow \frac{244}{333}$
   $0.4\dot{3} \rightarrow \frac{13}{30}$
2. $\frac{62}{495}$
3. a) $2\sqrt{6}$
   b) $5\sqrt{3}$
   c) $6\sqrt{3}$
   d) $6\sqrt{5}$

C
1. a) $\frac{6}{11}$
   b) $\frac{26}{990} = \frac{13}{495}$
2. a) 9
   b) $a = 4$
   c) $\frac{3}{5}$
3. $\frac{(5 + \sqrt{5})(2 - 2\sqrt{5})}{\sqrt{45}}$
   $= \frac{10 - 10\sqrt{5} + 2\sqrt{5} - 2(\sqrt{5})^2}{3\sqrt{5}}$
   $= \frac{-8\sqrt{5}}{3\sqrt{5}}$
   $= \frac{-8}{3}$
4. $\frac{61}{495}$
5. $19 - 8\sqrt{3}$
6. $\frac{\sqrt{125} + \sqrt{50}}{\sqrt{5}}$
   $= \frac{5\sqrt{5} + 5\sqrt{2}}{\sqrt{5}}$
   $= \frac{(5\sqrt{5} + 5\sqrt{2}) \times \sqrt{5}}{\sqrt{5} \quad \sqrt{5}}$
   $= \frac{5(\sqrt{5})^2 + 5\sqrt{10}}{5}$
   $= 5 + \sqrt{10}$

7 $1 + \sqrt{2}$
8 $\frac{25}{33}$

DIRECT AND INVERSE PROPORTION

A
1 d
2 a
3 b
4 c

B
1
a	**10**	12	30
b	2	**2.4**	6

2
x	2	4	**3**	5
y	12	**48**	27	75

3 a) $z = \frac{k}{v^2}$
   b) i) 62.5
      ii) $\frac{1}{2}$

C
1 $E = kF$
   $6 = k \times 15$
   $\therefore k = \frac{2}{5}$
   $E = \frac{2}{5}F$
   When F = 80 N, E = 32 cm
2 $V = kh^3$
   $60 = k \times 8$
   $k = 7.5$
   $V = 7.5h^3$
   $V = 937.5$ cm^3
3 $I = \frac{k}{d^2}$
   $50 = \frac{k}{4}$
   $\therefore k = 200$
   $I = \frac{200}{d^2}$
   a) $I = 16.3$ (1 d.p.)
   b) $d = 4$
4 $c = \frac{k}{b}$
   $\therefore 4 = \frac{k}{10}$ so $k = 40$
   Daisy is correct.

UPPER AND LOWER BOUNDS OF MEASUREMENT

A
1 b
2 c
3 c
4 b
5 d

B
1 a) 5.235
   b) 4.5
   c) 0.3245
   d) 8.44
2 Lower bound E
   Upper bound A

C
1 a) 7.9 cm
   b) 0.642 cm
2 Lower bound 3.9719 cm (5 s.f.)
   Upper bound 3.9738 cm (5 s.f.)
3 0.1811 g cm^{-3} ≤ density
   < 0.2 g cm^{-3}
4 11.25 cm^2
5 10.5%

ALGEBRA

ALGEBRA

A
1 d
2 c
3 d
4 a
5 c

B
1 $T = 6b + 0.67p$
2 a) 4
   b) 5
   c) 8
3 a) $5(2n + 3)$
   b) $12(2 - 3n)$
   c) $(n + 1)(n + 5)$
   d) $(n - 8)(n + 8)$
   e) $(n + 1)(n - 4)$
4 a) $b = \frac{p + 4}{3}$
   b) $b = \pm\sqrt{(4y + 6)}$
   c) $b = \frac{2 - 5n}{3}$

C
1 $V = 8.9$ (2 s.f.)
2 a) $4x + 7$
   b) i) $6(a + 2)$
      ii) $5a(2a - 3b)$
   c) i) $(n + 2)(n + 3)$
      ii) $\frac{2}{n + 2}$
3 $(n - 1)^2 + n + (n - 1)$
   $n^2 - 2n + 1 + n + n - 1$
   $= n^2 - 2n + 1 + 2n - 1$
   $= n^2$

EQUATIONS

A
1 c
2 d
3 b
4 c
5 a

B
1 a) $n = 5$
   b) $n = 36$
   c) $n = 7$
   d) $n = -5.5$
   e) $n = 25$
   f) $n = 4$
2 a) $n = 3$
   b) $n = 5$
   c) $n = 4$
   d) $n = 14$
3 a) $n = 0, n = 4$
   b) $n = -5, n = -1$
   c) $n = 3, n = 2$
   d) $n = -4, n = 7$
4 $2n + (n + 30°) + (n - 10°) = 180°$
   $4n + 20° = 180°$
   $n = 40°$

C
1 a) $m = 3$
   b) $p = 6/10$ or $p = 3/5$
   c) $x = 6$
   d) $\frac{3w + 2(3w + 2)}{6} = \frac{1}{3}$
   $3w + 6w + 4 = \frac{6}{3}$
   $3w + 6w + 4 = 2$
   $9w + 4 = 2$
   $w = \frac{-2}{9}$
2 a) $(x - 1)(x - 3)$
   b) $x = 1$ and $x = 3$
3 $k = \frac{3}{2}$ or 1.5
4 i) $k = 1$
   ii) $k = 4.5$

EQUATIONS AND INEQUALITIES

A
1 a
2 d
3 c
4 d
5 c

B
1 a) $a = 2, b = 4$
   b) $a = 3, b = 9$
   c) $a = 5, b = -2$
   d) $a = 3, b = -2$
2 5.6 and –3.6
3 a) $x < 2$
   b) $x \geq 6$
   c) $1 \leq x \leq 4$
   d) $\frac{1}{3} < x \leq 2$

C
1 a) –3 –2 –1 0 1 2
   b) $p \leq 2$
2 $x = 2.7$
3 $x = -3, y = 1.5$
4 a) $a = 8, b = 2$
   b) $a = 3, b = 2$

FURTHER ALGEBRA AND EQUATIONS

A
1 c
2 a
3 d
4 b
5 c

B
1 a) $(x + 6)(x + 5)$
   b) $\frac{4}{(x+6)} + \frac{4}{(x^2 + 11x + 30)}$
   $= \frac{4}{(x+6)} + \frac{4}{(x+6)(x+5)}$
   $= \frac{4(x+5) + 4}{(x+6)(x+5)}$
   $= \frac{4x + 24}{(x+6)(x+5)}$
   $= \frac{4}{(x+5)}$

2 a) $(x + 4)(x - 3) = 2$
      $x^2 + x - 12 = 2$
      $x^2 + x - 14 = 0$
   b) $x = 3.27$ or $x = -4.27$
3 $a = \frac{3(b + c)}{bc}$
   $abc = 3b + 3c$
   $abc - 3c = 3b$
   $c(ab - 3) = 3b$
   $\therefore c = \frac{3b}{ab - 3}$
   Greg is right.

C
1 a) $\frac{1}{2} \times (x - 3) \times (x + 4) = 12$
      $(x - 3)(x + 4) = 24$
      $x^2 + x - 12 = 24$
      $x^2 + x - 36 = 0$
   b) $x = 5.52$
      $\therefore$ Base of triangle is 2.52 cm
2 $a = \frac{8b + 5}{(4 - 3b)}$
   $a(4 - 3b) = 8b + 5$
   $4a - 3ab = 8b + 5$
   $4a - 5 = 8b + 3ab$
   $4a - 5 = b(8 + 3a)$
   $b = \frac{4a - 5}{8 + 3a}$
3 a) $a = 3, b = -6$
   b) Minimum value is –6.

STRAIGHT LINE GRAPHS

A
1 b
2 d
3 b
4 c
5 a

B
1 a), b) i)

   b) ii) $y = 3x + 2$
   c) (1, 5)
2 $y = 3 - 2x$ and $y = 4 - 2x$

C
1 a) Gradient $= -\frac{2}{3}$
   b) $3y + 2x = 6$ or $y = -\frac{2}{3}x + 2$
   c)

   d) (3, 2)
   e) $\frac{3}{2}$

CURVED GRAPHS

A
1 b
2 d
3 c
4 d
5 b

B
1 a)
x	–2	–1	0	1	2	3
y	6	1	–2	–3	–2	1

   b)

   c) i) $y = -3$
      ii) $x = 2.7, x = -0.62$

C
1 a)
x	–2	–1	0	1	2	3
	–12	–5	–4	–3	4	23

b)

c) i) $x = 1.6$
ii) $x = 2.4$
iii) $x = 1.8$
iv) $x = -1.4$

HARDER WORK ON GRAPHS

A
1 c
2 a
3 d
4 c

B
1 a) (2, 4)
b) (1, 7)
c) (6, 7)
d) (–2, 7)
e) (1, 7)
2 Statement is true since $x = 1$, $y = -4$ is a simultaneous solution of the two equations:
i.e. $2 \times 1 - (-4) = 6$
$1^2 + (-4)^2 = 17$

C
1 a) $x = 3$, $y = -5$ and $x = 5\frac{2}{5}$, $y = -2\frac{1}{5}$
b) They are the coordinates of the points where the line $3y = -12 - x$ intersects with the circle $x^2 + y^2 = 34$.
2 a)

b)

INTERPRETING GRAPHS

A
1 d
2 a
3 d

B
1 Vase A matches graph ii.
Vase B matches graph i.
Vase C matches graph iii.
2 a) Roots are $x = 3$ and $x = -2$ (read where curve crosses x axis)
b) i) Approximately, $x = 3.3$ and $x = -2.3$ (read across where $y = 2$)

ii) Approximately, $x = -2.7$ and $x = 2.6$ (draw the line $y = 1 - x$ and find the point of intersection with the curve)

C
1 a)

b) $a = 3$, $b = 5$
c) approximately 437
2 $a = 2$, $b = 3$

SHAPE, SPACE AND MEASURES

BEARINGS AND SCALE DRAWINGS

A
1 c
2 a
3 d
4 b

B
1 10 km
2 a)

b) 11.1 cm = 22.2 km
c) 098°
3 false

C
1 a) i) 325 m
ii) 060°
iii) 120°
b)

2 Lengths must be ± 2 mm.

TRANSFORMATIONS 1

A
1 a
2 c
3 b
4 b

B
1 a)
b)
c)

2 a) Translation
b) Rotation
c) Translation
d) Reflection

C
1 a) Reflection in the x axis.
b) Rotation 90° anticlockwise about (0, 0).
2

TRANSFORMATIONS 2

A
1 d
2 b
3 b

B
1 a) Reflection in the y axis
b) Rotation 90° clockwise about (0, 0)
c) Reflection in the line $y = x$
2

C
1

2 a) Translation by the vector $\binom{-12}{-4}$
b) Enlargement by a scale factor of $-\frac{1}{2}$, centre of enlargement at (0, 5)
c) Reflection in the line $y = 0$

SIMILARITY AND CONGRUENCY

A
1 c
2 b
3 b
4 b

B
1 a) n = 7.5 cm
b) n = 6.5 cm
c) n = 6.5 cm
d) n = 7.3 cm
2 a) Congruent (RHS)
b) Not congruent
c) Congruent (SSS)

C
1 a) i) angle XMN = 83°

ii) angle XNM = XẐY = 68°
Angles in a triangle add up to 180°. Therefore $180° - 68° - 29° = 83°$.
b) 3.65 cm
c) 11.74 cm
2 a) 225 cm²
b) 1.08 litres

LOCI AND COORDINATES IN 3D

A
1 c
2 d
3 a
4 d
5 b

B
1

2 R = (3, 0, 3), S = (3, 3, 1), T = (0, 3, 1), U = (0, 1, 1)

C
1

ANGLE PROPERTIES OF CIRCLES

A
1 c
2 a
3 d
4 a
5 c

B
1 a) a = 65°
b) a = 18°
c) a = 60°
d) a = 50°
e) a = 82°
2 John is correct. Angle a is 42° because angles in the same segment are equal.

C
1 a) 66°
b) The angle at the centre is twice that at the circumference. Hence $132° ÷ 2 = 66°$
2 a) angle ROQ = 140°
b) angle PRQ = 70°

ANSWERS

PYTHAGORAS' THEOREM

A
1. d
2. b
3. a
4. c

B
1. a) n = 15 cm
   b) n = 12.6 cm
   c) n = 15.1 cm
   d) n = 24.6 cm
2. Since $12^2 + 5^2 = 144 + 25 = 169 = 13^2$, the triangle must be right-angled for Pythagoras' Theorem to be applied.
3. Both statements are true.
   Length of line = $\sqrt{(6^2 + 3^2)}$
   = $\sqrt{45}$ in surd form.
   Midpoint = $\frac{(2+5)}{2}, \frac{(11+5)}{2}$
   = (3.5, 8)

C
1. $\sqrt{61}$ cm
2. 24.1 cm
3. 13.7 cm
4. $\sqrt{41}$ units

TRIGONOMETRY 1

A
1. a
2. b
3. d
4. a
5. c

B
1. a) n = 5 cm
   b) n = 6.3 cm
   c) n = 13.8 cm
   d) n = 14.9 cm
   e) n = 6.7 cm.
2. a) 38.7°
   b) 52.5°
   c) 23.6°

C
1. 15 cm
2. a) 9.9 cm
   b) 65°
3. 18 cm

TRIGONOMETRY 2

A
1. c
2. a
3. d
4. c
5. b

B
1. 068°
2. 13.8 cm (1 d.p.)
3. a) i) true
      ii) true
   b) 40.9° (1 d.p.)

C
1. 30.1°
2. a) 389.9 m (1d.p.)
   b) 14.6° (1d.p.)
   c) 22.5° (1 d.p.)

FURTHER TRIGONOMETRY

A
1. c
2. a
3. d
4. c

B
1. a) 13.2 cm (3 s.f.)
   b) 17.3 cm (3 s.f.)
   c) 32.5° (1 d.p.)
   d) 70.9° (1 d.p.)
2. Area = $\frac{1}{2} \times 18 \times 13 \times \sin 37°$
   = 70.4 cm^2
   Area is approximately 70 cm^2.
   Isobel is correct.
3. a) A (0°, 1), B (90°, 0), C (270°, 0), D (360°, 1)
   b)

C
1. a) 10.5 cm (3sf)
   b) 12.5 cm^2 (3sf)
   c) 42.5 cm^2 (3 s.f.)
2. 4.13 cm

MEASURES AND MEASUREMENT

A
1. b
2. d
3. a
4. d
5. c

B
1. a) 8000 m
   b) 3.25 kg
   c) 7000 kg
   d) 0.52 m
   e) 2700 ml
   f) 0.00262 km
2. 12.5 miles
3. 1.32 pounds
4. Lower limit = 46.5 metres
   Upper limit = 47.5 metres
5. 53.3 mph
6. 0.1 g/cm^{-3}

C
1. a) 17.6 pounds
   b) 48 kilometres
2. 80 kg
3. a) 1 hour 36 minutes
   b) 4.4 km/h
4. Length = 12.05 cm, width = 5.5 cm

AREA OF 2D SHAPES

A
1. c
2. d
3. b
4. d
5. b

B
1. a) false
   b) true
   c) true
   d) false
2. 38.6 cm
3. 84.21 cm^2

C
1. 81 cm^2
2. 38.8 cm
3. 16 cm (to nearest cm)
4. 120.24 cm^2

VOLUME OF 3D SHAPES

A
1. a
2. c
3. a
4. c
5. d

B
1. Emily is not correct. The correct volume is 345.6 ÷ 2, i.e. 172.8 cm^3.
2. 170.2 cm^3
3. 9.9 cm
4. 3807 cm^3
5. Volume needs three dimensions. V = 4pr^2 is only two-dimensional, hence must be a formula for area and not volume.

C
1. 64 cm^3
2. a) 672 cm^3
   b) 0.000672 m^3
3. 3.2 cm
4. $4r^2p$ volume
   $3\pi\sqrt{(r^2+p^2)}$ length
   $\frac{4\pi r^2}{3p}$ length

FURTHER LENGTH, AREA AND VOLUME

A
1. b
2. a
3. d
4. a
5. c

B
1. Solid A is 314 cm^3
   Solid B is 600 cm^3
   Solid C is 2 145 cm^3
   Solid D is 68 cm^3
2. The statement is false because:
   Area of segment
   = Area of sector – Area of triangle
   = 13.09 – 10.83
   = 2.26 cm^2

C
1. 73°
2. 0.0248 m^3 (3 s.f.)
3. 8 mm

VECTORS

A
1. b
2. c
3. a
4. d
5. b

B
1. a) true
   b) false
   c) true
   d) false
2. $\overrightarrow{OC} = 2\mathbf{a} - 3\mathbf{b}$, $\overrightarrow{OD} = 6(2\mathbf{a} - 3\mathbf{b})$
   Hence the vectors are parallel as one vector is a multiple of the other.
   The vectors lie on a straight line through O.

3.
   a) $\mathbf{a} + \mathbf{b} = \binom{-1}{8}$
   b) $\mathbf{a} + \mathbf{b} = \binom{3}{-1}$

C
1. $\overrightarrow{AB} = -3\mathbf{a} + 3\mathbf{b}$, $\overrightarrow{CD} = -5\mathbf{a} + 5\mathbf{b}$
   Since $\overrightarrow{AB} = \frac{3}{5}\overrightarrow{CD}$, then AB and CD are parallel.
2. a) $\overrightarrow{AC} = \mathbf{a} + \mathbf{b}$
   b) $\overrightarrow{BD} = \mathbf{b} + 2\mathbf{a} - \mathbf{a}$
   = $3\mathbf{b} - \mathbf{a}$
   hence $\overrightarrow{AD} = \overrightarrow{AB} + \overrightarrow{BD}$
   = $\mathbf{a} + 3\mathbf{b} - \mathbf{a}$
   $\overrightarrow{AD} = 3\mathbf{b}$
   $\overrightarrow{AD} = 3\overrightarrow{BC}$, so BC is parallel to AD.
   c) $\overrightarrow{AN} = \overrightarrow{AD} + \overrightarrow{DN}$
   = $3\mathbf{b} - \frac{1}{2}(2\mathbf{b} - \mathbf{a})$
   = $3\mathbf{b} - \mathbf{b} + \frac{1}{2}\mathbf{a}$
   = $\frac{1}{2}\mathbf{a} + 2\mathbf{b}$
   d) $\overrightarrow{YD} = \overrightarrow{YA} + \overrightarrow{AD}$
   = $-\frac{3}{4}(\frac{1}{2}\mathbf{a} + 2\mathbf{b}) + 3\mathbf{b}$
   = $-\frac{3}{8}\mathbf{a} - \frac{3}{2}\mathbf{b} + 3\mathbf{b}$
   = $-\frac{3}{8}\mathbf{a} + \frac{3}{2}\mathbf{b}$
   = $\frac{3}{8}(4\mathbf{b} - \mathbf{a})$

HANDLING DATA

COLLECTING DATA

A
1. b
2. d
3. a
4. b
5. d

B
1. The tick boxes overlap. Which box would somebody who did 2 hours of homework tick? It also needs an extra box with 5 or more hours.

   How much time do you spend to the nearest hour, doing homework each night?

   0 up to 1 hour
   1 up to 2 hours
   2 up to 3 hours
   4 up to 5 hours
   5 hours and over

2. Year   7:   15 students
             8:   22 students
             9:   20 students
            10:   24 students
            11:   19 students

C
1. From the list below, tick your favourite chocolate bar.
   Mars   ☐
   Twix   ☐
   Toblerone   ☐
   Galaxy   ☐
   Bounty   ☐
   Snickers   ☐
   other ....

ANSWERS

2 The key to this question is to break it into subgroups.
  a) On average, how many hours per school day do you watch television?
  0 up to 1 hour ☐
  1 up to 2 hours ☐
  2 up to 3 hours ☐
  3 up to 4 hours ☐
  Over 4 hours ☐
  b) On average, how many hours at the weekend do you watch television?
  0 up to 2 hours ☐
  2 up to 4 hours ☐
  4 up to 6 hours ☐
  6 up to 8 hours ☐
  Over 8 hours ☐
3 a) 30 students
  b) 14 girls

SCATTER DIAGRAMS AND CORRELATION

A
1 c
2 a
3 b

B
1 a) Positive correlation
  b) Negative correlation
  c) Positive correlation
  d) No correlation
2 a) Positive correlation
  b) [scatter graph: mathematics (%) vs physics (%), line of best fit]
  c) 74% approximately

C
1 a) [scatter graph: Age (in years) vs Number of hours sleep, line of best fit]
  b) Negative correlation – the younger the child, the more hours sleep they needed.
  c) Line of best fit on diagram above.
  d) A four-year-old child needs approximately 14 hours sleep.
  e) This only gives an estimate as it follows the trend of the data. Similarly, if you continued the line it would assume that you may eventually need no hours sleep at a certain age, which is not the case.

AVERAGES 1

A
1 c
2 b
3 d
4 d
5 b

B
1 a) false
  b) true
  c) false
  d) true
2 a) mean = 141.35
  b) The manufacturer is justified in making this claim since the mean is just over 141, and the mode and median are also approximately 141.
3 $x = 17$

C
1 4.65
2 81
3 £440
4 $3.\dot{3}, 4.\dot{6}, 3.\dot{6}, 3, 2.\dot{3}$

AVERAGES 2

A
1 c
2 b
3 a
4 a

B
1 21.5 mm
2 a) 47
  b) 35
  c) 40

C
1 1 | 2 4 9 5 7 5 8 8
   2 | 2 7 3 5 7 7
   3 | 1 6 5 2 8
   4 | 1
   Reordering gives this.
   1 | 2 4 5 5 7 8 8 9
   2 | 2 3 5 7 7 7
   3 | 1 2 5 6 8
   4 | 1
   Key: 1|2 means 12
   Stem: 10 minutes
2 a) £31.80
  b) This is only an estimate because the midpoint of the data has been used.
  c) $30 \leq x < 40$

CUMULATIVE FREQUENCY GRAPHS

A
1 c
2 d
3 c
4 a

B
1 a)

Examination mark	Frequency	Cumulative frequency
0–10	4	4
11–20	6	10
21–30	11	21
31–40	24	45
41–50	18	63
51–60	7	70
61–70	3	73

b) [cumulative frequency graph: Marks vs Cumulative frequency]

c) 36.5
d) 43 – 28 = 15 marks
e) 45.5 marks

C
1 a)

Time (nearest minute)	Frequency	Cumulative frequency
$120 < t \leq 140$	1	1
$140 < t \leq 160$	8	9
$160 < t \leq 180$	24	33
$180 < t \leq 200$	29	62
$200 < t \leq 220$	10	72
$220 < t \leq 240$	5	77
$240 < t \leq 260$	3	80

b) [cumulative frequency graph: Time (nearest minute) vs Cumulative frequency]

c) i) Interquartile range = 198 – 169 = 29 minutes
   ii) 80 – 65 = 15 runners
d) [box plot showing Lower quartile, Median, Upper quartile across Time (nearest minute)]

HISTOGRAMS

A
1 d
2 b
3 b
4 a

B
1 a) $5 < t \leq 15$ 26
     $20 < t \leq 30$ 14
  b) [histogram: Time (minutes) vs Frequency density]

C

1

(Histogram: Frequency density vs Weight (W kg))

2

Length S (in seconds)	Frequency
$0 \leq S < 10$	2
$10 \leq S < 15$	5
$15 \leq S < 20$	21
$20 \leq S < 40$	28
$S \geq 40$	0

PROBABILITY

A
1. d
2. c
3. b
4. a
5. d

B
1. a)

	\multicolumn{4}{c}{Spinner 1}
Spinner 2		1	2	3	3
	1	2	3	4	4
	2	3	4	5	5
	3	4	5	6	6
	6	7	8	9	9

   b) i) $\frac{4}{16} = \frac{1}{4}$
   ii) $\frac{2}{16} = \frac{1}{8}$
   iii) 0

2. 0.09

3. a) $\frac{49}{169}$
   b) $\frac{84}{169}$

C
1. a) i) 0.35
   ii) 0
   b) 50 red beads

2. a) $\frac{6}{36} = \frac{1}{6}$
   b) $\frac{4}{36} = \frac{1}{9}$

3. a)

Monopoly
- 0.4........ Kevin wins
- 0.6........ Nathan wins

Pool
- 0.3........ Kevin wins
- 0.7........ Nathan wins
- 0.3........ Kevin wins
- 0.7........ Nathan wins

   b) 0.42
   c) 0.46

LETTS EDUCATIONAL
The Chiswick Centre
414 Chiswick High Road
London W4 5TF
Tel: 020 8996 3333
Fax: 020 8742 8390
Email: mail@lettsed.co.uk
Website: www.letts-education.com

C These are GCSE style questions. Answer all parts of the questions. Show your workings (on separate paper if necessary) and include the correct units in your answers.

1 Enlarge triangle N by scale factor $\frac{1}{3}$ with centre R (–6, 7)

(3 marks)

2 The diagram shows four triangles, T_1, T_2, T_3 and T_4.

Describe fully the single transformation that maps:

a) T_1 onto T_2 .... (2 marks)

b) T_1 onto T_3 .... (2 marks)

c) T_1 onto T_4 .... (2 marks)

Score / 9

How well did you do?
1–4 marks Try again
5–9 marks Getting there
10–16 marks Good work
17–21 marks Excellent!

TOTAL SCORE / 21

For more information on this topic see pages 62–63 of your Success Guide.

SIMILARITY AND CONGRUENCY

A
Choose just one answer, a, b, c or d.

1 These two shapes are similar. What is the size of angle x?

a) 90° b) 47°
c) 53° d) 50° (1 mark)

2 What is the length of y in the triangles above?
a) 14 cm
b) 12 cm
c) 8 cm
d) 16 cm (1 mark)

3 These two shapes are similar. What is the radius of the smaller cone?

Diagrams not drawn to scale

a) 2 cm b) 3.12 cm
c) 4 cm d) 5 cm (1 mark)

4 What is the perpendicular height of the larger cone above?
a) 12 cm
b) 9.16 cm
c) 10.47 cm
d) 10 cm (1 mark)

Score / 4

B
Answer all parts of the questions.

1 Calculate the lengths marked n in these similar shapes. Give your answers correct to 1 decimal place.

a) n = ... (2 marks)
b) n = ... (2 marks)
c) n = ... (2 marks)
d) n = ... (2 marks)

2 Which of the following pairs of triangles, C and D, are congruent? For those that are, state whether the reason is SSS, RHS, SAS or AAS.

a) .... b) .... c) .... (3 marks)

Score / 11

C These are GCSE style questions. Answer all parts of the questions. Show your workings (on separate paper if necessary) and include the correct units in your answers.

1 In the diagram MN is parallel to YZ.

YMX and ZNX are straight lines.

XM = 5.1 cm, XY = 9.5 cm, XN = 6.3 cm, YZ = 6.8 cm.

$\angle YXZ = 29°$, $\angle XZY = 68°$.

Diagrams not accurately drawn

a) i) Calculate the size of angle XMN. .... ° (1 mark)

ii) Explain how you obtained your answer.

....

.... (1 mark)

b) Calculate the length of MN. ....

.... cm (2 marks)

c) Calculate the length of XZ. ....

.... cm (2 marks)

2 Soup is sold in two similar cylindrical cans.

90 cm   150 cm

a) The area of the label on the smaller can is 81 cm²

Calculate the area of the label on the larger can. (The labels are also similar and in the same proportion as the height of the cans.)

.... (2 marks)

b) The capacity of the larger can of soup is 5 litres.

Calculate the capacity of the smaller can of soup.

.... (2 marks)

Score   / 10

How well did you do?
1–6 marks   Try again
7–12 marks Getting there
13–18 marks Good work
19–25 marks Excellent!

TOTAL SCORE   /25

For more information on this topic see pages 64–65 of your Success Guide.

LOCI AND COORDINATES IN 3D

A

Choose just one answer, a, b, c or d.

1 What shape would be formed if the locus of all the points from a fixed point P is drawn?
a) rectangle   b) square
c) circle   d) kite   (1 mark)

Questions 2–5 refer to the diagram opposite.

2 What are the coordinates of point A?
a) (4, 3, 1)   b) (4, 3, 0)
c) (0, 3, 1)   d) (4, 0, 1)   (1 mark)

3 What are the coordinates of point B?
a) (0, 3, 1)   b) (0, 0, 0)
c) (4, 3, 0)   d) (0, 3, 0)   (1 mark)

4 What are the coordinates of point C?
a) (0, 3, 1)   b) (4, 3, 1)
c) (4, 0, 0)   d) (4, 3, 0)   (1 mark)

5 What are the coordinates of point D?
a) (4, 3, 0)   b) (4, 3, 1)
c) (0, 0, 0)   d) (0, 3, 0)   (1 mark)

Score / 5

B

Answer all parts of the questions.

1 The diagram shows the position of the post office (P), the hospital (H) and the school (S). Robert lives less than 4 miles away from the hospital, less than 5 miles away from the post office and less than 8 miles away from the school. Show by shading the area where Robert can live.

Use a scale of 1 cm = 2 miles.

(4 marks)

2 The diagram shows a solid. Complete the coordinates for each of the vertices listed below.

R = (.... , ... , ...)
S = (.... , ... , ...)
T = (.... , ... , ...)
U = (.... , ... , ...)

(4 marks)

Score / 8

52

C This is a GCSE style question. Answer all parts of the question. Show all your workings (on separate sheets of paper if necessary) and include the correct units in your answers.

1 In this question you should use ruler and compasses only for the constructions.

Triangle ABC is an adventure playground, drawn to a scale of 1 cm to 20 m.

Diagram accurately drawn to scale of 1 cm to 20 m

a) On the diagram, draw accurately the locus of the points which are 100 m from C. (2 marks)

b) On the diagram, draw accurately the locus of the points which are the same distance from A as they are from C. (2 marks)

c) P is an ice cream kiosk inside the adventure playground.

P is the same distance from A as it is from C.

P is the same distance from AC as it is from AB.

On the diagram, mark the point P clearly with a cross.

Label it with the letter P. (3 marks)

Score / 7

How well did you do?
1–4 marks   Try again
5–9 marks   Getting there
10–14 marks Good work
15–20 marks Excellent!

TOTAL SCORE   / 20

For more information on this topic see page 66 of your Success Guide.

LOCI AND COORDINATES IN 3D

53

ANGLE PROPERTIES OF CIRCLES

A

Choose just one answer, a, b, c or d.
Questions 1–5 refer to the diagrams drawn below.

Diagram A: circle with inscribed quadrilateral, angles labelled b, a, 80°, 110°.

Diagram B: circle with triangle through centre O, angle 70° at top, angles d and c marked.

Diagram C: circle with centre O, triangle with angle e marked.

1 In diagram A, what is the size of angle a?
 a) 80°   b) 110°
 c) 100°   d) 70°   (1 mark)

2 In diagram A, what is the size of angle b?
 a) 70°   b) 110°
 c) 100°   d) 80°   (1 mark)

3 In diagram B, what is the size of angle c?
 a) 35°   b) 70°
 c) 100°   d) 140°   (1 mark)

4 In diagram B, what is the size of angle d?
 a) 70°   b) 35°
 c) 100°   d) 140°   (1 mark)

5 In diagram C, what is the size of angle e?
 a) 100°   b) 45°
 c) 90°   d) 110°   (1 mark)

Score / 5

B

Answer all parts of the questions.

1 Some angles are written on cards. Match the missing angles in the diagrams below with the correct card. O represents the centre of the circle.

| 50° | 60° | 82° | 65° | 18° |

a) Circle with centre O, tangent, angle 65°, angle a.
b) Circle with centre O, tangent, angle 72°, angle a.
c) Circle with centre O, angle 120°, angle a.
d) Circle with centre O, external angle 65°, angle a.
e) Cyclic quadrilateral, angle 82°, angle a.

(5 marks)

2 John says that 'angle a is 42°'.

Diagram: circle with angle 42° and angle a.

Explain whether John is correct.

....
(1 mark)

Score / 6

C These are GCSE style questions. Answer all parts of the questions. Show your workings (on separate paper if necessary) and include the correct units in your answers.

1

R, S and T are points on the circumference of a circle with centre O.

a) Find angle RST.

.... °   (1 mark)

b) Give a reason for your answer.

....
....   (2 marks)

2

PQ and PR are tangents to a circle centre O.

Point S is a point on the circumference.

Angle RSQ is 70°.

a) Find angle ROQ, marked $x°$ in the diagram.

.... °   (2 marks)

b) Find the size of angle PRQ, marked $y°$ in the diagram.

....
....
....
.... °   (4 marks)

Score   / 9

How well did you do?
1–2 marks   Try again
3–6 marks   Getting there
7–12 marks   Good work
13–20 marks   Excellent!

TOTAL SCORE   / 20

For more information on this topic see page 67 of your Success Guide.

ANGLE PROPERTIES OF CIRCLES

PYTHAGORAS' THEOREM

A

Choose just one answer, a, b, c or d.

1 What is the name of the longest side of a right-angled triangle?
 a) hypo   b) hippopotamus
 c) crocodile   d) hypotenuse   (1 mark)

2 Calculate the missing length y of this triangle.

 a) 169 cm   b) 13 cm
 c) 17 cm   d) 84.5 cm   (1 mark)

3 Calculate the missing length y of this triangle.
 a) 13.2 cm   b) 5 cm
 c) 25 cm   d) 625 cm   (1 mark)

4 Point A has coordinates (1, 4), point B has coordinates (4, 10). What are the coordinates of the midpoint of the line AB?
 a) (5, 14)   b) (3, 6)
 c) (2.5, 7)   d) (1.5, 3)   (1 mark)

Score / 4

B

Answer all parts of the questions.

1 Calculate the missing lengths of these right-angled triangles. Give your answer to 3 significant figures, where appropriate.

a) [9cm, 12cm, n]
b) [15.2cm, 8.5cm, n]
c) [12.1cm, 9cm, n]
d) [31cm, 18.9cm, n]

n = ... cm n = ... cm n = ... cm n = ... cm

(2 marks)   (2 marks)   (2 marks)   (2 marks)

2 Molly says, 'The angle $x°$ in this triangle is 90°.'

Explain how Molly knows this without measuring the size of the angle.

....
....

(2 marks)

3 Colin says, 'The length of this line is $\sqrt{45}$ units and the coordinates of the midpoint are (3.5, 8).'

Decide whether these statements are true or false. Give an explanation for your answer.

....
....

(5, 11)
(2, 5)

(2 marks)

Score / 12

56

These are GCSE style questions. Answer all parts of the questions. Show your workings (on separate paper if necessary) and include the correct units in your answers.

1 ABC is a right-angled triangle.

AB = 5 cm, BC = 6 cm.

Calculate the length of AC.

Leave your answer in surd form.

.... cm   (3 marks)

2 Calculate the length of the diagonal of this rectangle. Give your answer to one decimal place.

.... cm   (3 marks)

3 Calculate the perpendicular height of the isosceles triangle. Give your answer to one decimal place.

.... m   (3 marks)

4 Calculate the length of AB in this diagram. Leave your answer in surd form.

A (3, 5)
B (7, 10)
Diagram not drawn to scale

....   (3 marks)

Score   / 12

How well did you do?
1–7 marks   Try again
8–14 marks   Getting there
15–21 marks   Good work
22–28 marks   Excellent!

TOTAL SCORE   / 28

For more information on this topic see pages 68–69 of your Success Guide.

TRIGONOMETRY 1

A
Choose just one answer, a, b, c or d.
Questions 1–5 refer to this diagram.

[Triangle with P at top, Q at bottom-left (right angle), R at bottom-right. PQ = 3cm, PR = 5cm, QR = 4cm, angle x at R.]

1 Which length is the opposite to angle x?
 a) PQ   b) PR   c) QR   d) RX
(1 mark)

2 Which length of the triangle is the hypotenuse?
 a) PQ   b) PR   c) QR   d) RX
(1 mark)

3 Which fraction represents tan x?
 a) $\frac{3}{5}$ b) $\frac{4}{3}$ c) $\frac{4}{5}$ d) $\frac{3}{4}$
(1 mark)

4 Which fraction represents sin x?
 a) $\frac{3}{5}$ b) $\frac{4}{3}$ c) $\frac{5}{3}$ d) $\frac{4}{5}$
(1 mark)

5 Which fraction represents cos x?
 a) $\frac{3}{5}$ b) $\frac{3}{4}$ c) $\frac{4}{5}$ d) $\frac{5}{4}$
(1 mark)

Score / 5

B
Answer all parts of the questions.

1 Choose a card for each of the missing lengths n on the triangles. The lengths have been rounded to 1 decimal place.

Cards: 6.3 cm | 6.7 cm | 13.8 cm | 5 cm | 14.9 cm

a) [triangle, n, 10cm, 30°]   b) [triangle, n, 12.5cm, 60°]   c) [triangle, 10cm, 36°, n]   d) [triangle, 14cm, 20°, n]   e) [triangle, 6cm, 48°, n]

n = ... cm   n = ... cm   n = ... cm   n = ... cm   n = ... cm

(5 marks)

2 Work out the missing angle x in the diagrams below.
Give your answers to 1 decimal place.

a) [triangle, 12cm, 15cm, x]   b) [triangle, 14cm, 23cm, x]   c) [triangle, 25cm, 10cm, x]

x = ... ° x = ... ° x = ... °

(2 marks)   (2 marks)   (2 marks)

Score / 11

C These are GCSE style questions. Answer all parts of the questions. Show your workings (on separate paper if necessary) and include the correct units in your answers.

1 RS and SU are two sides of a rectangle.

T is a point on SU.

SU is 50 cm.

ST is 18 cm.

Angle STR is 40°.

Calculate the width of the rectangle.

Give your answer correct to the nearest centimetre.

.... cm

Diagram not drawn to scale

(3 marks)

2 The diagram shows two triangles PQR and QRS.

Not to scale

a) Calculate the length of QR.

.... cm (2 marks)

b) Calculate angle QPR.

.... ° (3 marks)

3 The diagram shows a right-angled triangle ABC.

Diagram not drawn to scale

Calculate the length of AC.

.... cm

(3 marks)

Score   / 11

How well did you do?
1–7 marks   Try again
8–12 marks Getting there
13–19 marks Good work
20–27 marks Excellent!

TOTAL SCORE   / 27

For more information on this topic see pages 70–71 of your Success Guide.

TRIGONOMETRY 2

A
Choose just one answer, a, b, c or d.

Questions 1–3 refer to this diagram.

Questions 4 and 5 refer to this diagram.

1 Calculate the value of x.
 a) 13 cm b) 8.7 cm
 c) 7.5 cm d) 10 cm (1 mark)

2 Calculate the value of y.
 a) 13 cm b) 8.7 cm
 c) 7.5 cm d) 10 cm (1 mark)

3 Which fraction represents cos P?
 a) $\frac{13}{15}$ b) $\frac{3}{4}$
 c) $\frac{3}{5}$ d) $\frac{1}{2}$ (1 mark)

4 Calculate the size of angle a to the nearest degree.
 a) 53° b) 45° c) 39° d) 37° (1 mark)

5 Calculate the length of b to the nearest centimetre.
 a) 9 cm b) 19 cm
 c) 29 cm d) 16 cm (1 mark)

Score / 5

B
Answer all parts of the questions.

1 A ship sails 20 km due north and then 50 km due east. What is the bearing of the finishing point from the starting point?

Bearing .... ° (2 marks)

2 The diagram represents the sector of a circle with centre O and radius 12 cm. Angle POR equals 70°.

Calculate the length of the straight line PR.

.... cm (3 marks)

3 CDEFGH is a right-angled triangular prism.

N is the midpoint of DE.

a) Decide whether the following statements are true or false.

 i) The length HD is 19.2 cm, correct to 3 s.f. ....

 ii) The size of angle HDC is 51.3°, correct to 1 decimal place. .... (2 marks)

b) Calculate the size of angle HNC. .... ° (3 marks)

Score / 10

60

C These are GCSE style questions. Answer all parts of the questions. Show your workings (on separate paper if necessary) and include the correct units in your answers.

1 The diagram shows a triangle PQR.

PS = 6.5 cm, QR = 12.7 cm and angle QRS = 62°.

Calculate the size of the angle marked $x°$.

Give your answer correct to 1 decimal place.

....

....° (5 marks)

2 R, S and T are three points on horizontal ground.

R is 1500 m due west of S and
T is 1200 m due south of C.

SP is a vertical tower.

The angle of elevation of P from T is 18°.

a) Calculate the height of the mast.

....

.... m (2 marks)

b) Find the angle of elevation of P from R.

....

....° (2 marks)

c) V is a point on RT which is nearest to S.

Calculate the angle of elevation of P from V.

....

....

....

....° (5 marks)

Score   / 14

How well did you do?
1–8 marks   Try again
9–14 marks   Getting there
15–21 marks   Good work
22–29 marks   Excellent!

TOTAL SCORE   / 29

For more information on this topic see pages 72–73 of your Success Guide.

FURTHER TRIGONOMETRY

A

Choose just one answer, a, b, c or d.

1. If sin x = 0.5, what is a possible value of x?
   a) 180°
   b) 120°
   c) 150°
   d) 90° (1 mark)

2. If cos x = 0.5, what is a possible value of x?
   a) 300°
   b) 150°
   c) 65°
   d) 120° (1 mark)

3. If sin $x = \frac{\sqrt{3}}{2}$, what is a possible value of x?
   a) 320°
   b) 400°
   c) 360°
   d) 420° (1 mark)

4. Which is the correct formula for the cosine rule?
   a) $a^2 = b^2 - c^2 + 2bc \cos A$
   b) $b^2 = a^2 + c^2 - 2bc \cos B$
   c) $a^2 = b^2 + c^2 - 2bc \cos A$
   d) $c^2 = b^2 + a^2 - 2ab \cos A$ (1 mark)

Score / 4

B

Answer all parts of the questions.

1. Calculate the missing lengths or angles in the diagrams below.

   a) x = ... cm (2 marks)
   b) x = ... cm (2 marks)
   c) x = ... ° (2 marks)
   d) x = ... ° (2 marks)

2. Isobel says, 'The area of this triangle is 70 cm².'

   Decide, with working to justify your answer, whether this statement is true or false.

   ....
   ....
   (2 marks)

3. The diagram shows a sketch of part of the curve y = f(x), where f(x) = cos x°.

   a) Write down the coordinates of points:

   A (......... , ...)   B (......... , ...)   C (......... , ...)   D (......... , ...)   (4 marks)

   b) On the same diagram, sketch the graph of y = cos 2x (3 marks)

Score / 17

C These are GCSE style questions. Answer all parts of the questions. Show your workings (on separate paper if necessary) and include the correct units in your answers.

1 The diagram shows a quadrilateral PQRS.

PS = 4.3 cm, PQ = 5.8 cm, SR = 7.3 cm.

Angle PSR = 127°, angle PQR = 54°.

a) Calculate the length of PR.

Give your answer correct to 3 significant figures. ....

.... cm (3 marks)

b) Calculate the area of triangle PRS.

Give your answer correct to 3 significant figures. ....

.... cm² (2 marks)

c) Calculate the area of the quadrilateral PQRS.

Give your answer correct to 3 significant figures. ....

....

.... cm² (6 marks)

2

In triangle VWX, Y is the point on WX such that VW = VY.

VW = 6.3 cm, VX = 12.3 cm, XY = 8.7 cm.

Calculate the length of WY. ....

....

.... cm (5 marks)

Score / 16

How well did you do?
1–10 marks Try again
11–19 marks Getting there
20–27 marks Good work
28–37 marks Excellent!

TOTAL SCORE / 37

For more information on this topic see pages 74–75 of your Success Guide.

MEASURES AND MEASUREMENT

A Choose just one answer, a, b, c or d.

1. What is 2 500 g in kilograms?
   a) 25 kg
   b) 2.5 kg
   c) 0.25 kg
   d) 250 kg (1 mark)

2. Approximately how many pounds are in 4 kg?
   a) 6.9
   b) 12.4
   c) 7.7
   d) 8.8 (1 mark)

3. Jessica is 165 cm tall to the nearest cm. What is the lower limit of her height?
   a) 164.5 cm
   b) 165.5 cm
   c) 165 cm
   d) 164.9 cm (1 mark)

4. What is the volume of a piece of wood with a density of 680 kg m^{-3} and a mass of 34 kg?
   a) 0.5 m^3
   b) 20 m^3
   c) 2 m^3
   d) 0.05 m^3 (1 mark)

5. A car travels for two and a half hours at a speed of 42 mph. How far does the car travel?
   a) 96 miles
   b) 100 miles
   c) 105 miles
   d) 140 miles (1 mark)

Score / 5

B Answer all parts of the questions.

1. Complete the statements below.
   a) 8 km = ... m
   b) 3 250 g = ... kg
   c) 7 tonnes = ... kg
   d) 52 cm = ... m
   e) 2.7 l = ... ml
   e) 262 cm = ... km (6 marks)

2. Two towns are approximately 20 km apart. How many miles is this?
   .... (1 mark)

3. A recipe uses 600 g of flour. Approximately how many pounds is this?
   .... (1 mark)

4. A field is 47 metres long to the nearest metre. Write down the upper and lower limits of the length of the field.
   .... (2 marks)

5. Giovanni drove 200 miles in 3 hours and 45 minutes. At what average speed did he travel?
   .... (2 marks)

6. What is the density of a toy if its mass is 200 g and its volume is 2000 cm^3?
   .... (2 marks)

Score / 14

C These are GCSE style questions. Answer all parts of the questions. Show your workings (on separate paper if necessary) and include the correct units in your answers.

1 a) Change 8 kilograms into pounds.

.... pounds (2 marks)

b) Change 30 miles into kilometres.

.... km (2 marks)

2 Two solids each have a volume of 2.5m^3.

The density of solid A is 320 kg per m^3.

The density of solid B is 288 kg per m^3.

Calculate the difference in the masses of the solids. .... kg (3 marks)

3 Amy took part in a sponsored walk.

She walked from the school to the park and back.

The distance from the school to the park is 8 km.

a) Amy walked from the school to the park at an average speed of 5 km/h.

Find the time she took to walk from the school to the park.

.... (2 marks)

b) Her average speed for the return journey was 4 km/h.

Calculate her average speed for the whole journey.

.... km/h (4 marks)

4 The length of the rectangle is 12.1 cm to the nearest mm.

The width of the rectangle is 6 cm to the nearest cm.

Write down the lower limits for the length and width of the rectangle.

Length .... cm

Width .... cm

(2 marks)

Score / 15

How well did you do?
1–11 marks Try again
12–19 marks Getting there
20–27 marks Good work
28–34 marks Excellent!

TOTAL SCORE / 34

For more information on this topic see pages 76–77 of your Success Guide.

AREA OF 2D SHAPES

A Choose just one answer, a, b, c or d.

1 What is the area of this triangle?

(triangle: height 8 cm, base 15 cm)

a) 60 mm² b) 120 cm²
c) 60 cm² d) 46 cm²   (1 mark)

2 What is the approximate circumference of a circle of radius 4 cm?

a) 25.1 cm² b) 50.3 cm
c) 12.6 cm d) 25.1 cm   (1 mark)

3 Change 50 000 cm² into m².

a) 500 m² b) 5 m²
c) 0.5 m² d) 50 m²   (1 mark)

4 What is the area of this circle?

(circle: radius 4 cm)

a) 25.1 cm² b) 55 cm²
c) 12.6 cm² d) 50.3 cm²   (1 mark)

5 If the area of a rectangle is 20 cm² and its width is 2.5 cm, what is the length of the rectangle?

a) 9 cm   b) 8 cm   c) 7.5 cm   d) 2.5 cm
(1 mark)

Score / 5

B Answer all parts of the questions.

1 For each of the diagrams below, decide whether the area given is true or false.

a) (triangle: 6 cm, 8 cm)
b) (parallelogram: 6 cm, 10 cm)
c) (circle: 15 cm)
d) (trapezium: 6 cm top, 9 cm bottom, 4 cm height)

a) Area = 48 cm² .... (1 mark)

b) Area = 60 cm² .... (1 mark)

c) Area = 177 cm² .... (1 mark)

d) Area = 108 cm² .... (1 mark)

2 Calculate the perimeter of this shape.

(semicircle: diameter 15 cm)

.... cm   (3 marks)

3 Calculate the area of the shaded region.

(rectangle 12.6 cm × 7.2 cm with triangular cut-out: base 4.2 cm, height 3.1 cm)

.... cm²   (3 marks)

Score / 10

C These are GCSE style questions. Answer all parts of the questions. Show your workings (on separate paper if necessary) and include the correct units in your answers.

1 Work out the area of the shape shown in the diagram.

State the units with your answer.

....
....
....
....
....
....

Diagrams not drawn to scale

(5 marks)

2 Calculate the perimeter of the shape shown in the diagram.

Give your answer to 3 significant figures.

....
....
....
....
....
.... cm

(3 marks)

3 The area of a circular sewing pattern is 200 cm²

Calculate the diameter of the sewing pattern. Give your answer correct to the nearest centimetre.

....
.... cm (4 marks)

4 Calculate the area of the shape.

State the units with your answer.

....
....
....
....

(3 marks)

Score   / 15

How well did you do?
1–8 marks   Try again
9–14 marks   Getting there
15–22 marks   Good work
23–30 marks   Excellent!

TOTAL SCORE   / 30

For more information on this topic see pages 78–79 of your Success Guide.

AREA OF 2D SHAPES

67

VOLUME OF 3D SHAPES

A Choose just one answer, a, b, c or d.

1 What is the volume of this cuboid?
a) 30 cm³
b) 16 cm³
c) 300 mm³
d) 15 cm³

(1 mark)

2 What is the volume of this prism?
a) 64 cm³
b) 240 cm³
c) 120 cm³
d) 20 cm³

(1 mark)

3 The volume of a cuboid is 20 cm³. If its height is 1 cm and its width is 4 cm, what is its length?
a) 5 cm   b) 10 cm
c) 15 cm   d) 8 cm   (1 mark)

4 A cube of volume 2 cm³ is enlarged by a scale factor of 3. What is the volume of the enlarged cube?
a) 6 cm³   b) 27 cm³
c) 54 cm³   d) 18 cm³   (1 mark)

5 If p and q represent lengths, decide what the formula $\frac{3}{5}\pi p^2 q$ shows.
a) circumference   b) length
c) area   d) volume   (1 mark)

Score / 5

B Answer all parts of the questions.

1 Emily says: 'The volume of this prism is 345.6 m³'

Decide whether Emily is correct. Show working out to justify your answer.

....

....

(1 mark)

2 Calculate the volume of the cylinder, clearly stating your units.

....

....

(2 marks)

3 If the volume of both solids is the same, work out the height of the cylinder to 1 decimal place.

....cm   (4 marks)

4 The volume of a cube is 141 cm³

Each length of the cube is enlarged by a scale factor of 3. What is the volume of the enlarged cube?

.... cm³   (2 marks)

5 Lucy says that 'The volume of a sphere is given by the formula $V = 4\pi r^2$'. Explain why she cannot be correct.

....

(1 mark)

Score / 10

C These are GCSE style questions. Answer all parts of the questions. Show your workings (on separate paper if necessary) and include the correct units in your answers.

1 A cube has a surface area of 96 cm². Work out the volume of the cube.

....
(4 marks)

2 A door wedge is in the shape of a prism with cross section VWXY.

VW = 7 cm, VY = 0.15 m, WX = 9 cm.

The width of the door wedge is 0.08 m.

a) Calculate the volume of the door wedge.

.... cm³ (3 marks)

b) What is the volume of the door wedge in m³?

.... m³ (1 mark)

3 The volume of this cylinder is 250 cm³.

The height of the cylinder is 8 cm.

Calculate the radius of the cylinder giving your answer to 1 decimal place.

.... cm (3 marks)

4 Here are three expressions.

Expression	Length	Area	Volume
$4r^2p$			
$3\pi\sqrt{(r^2 + p^2)}$			
$\dfrac{4\pi r^2}{3p}$			

r and p are lengths.

Put a tick in the correct column to show whether the expression can be used for length, area or volume.

(3 marks)

Score   / 14

How well did you do?
1–7 marks Try again
8–14 marks Getting there
15–22 marks Good work
23–29 marks Excellent!

TOTAL SCORE   / 29

For more information on this topic see pages 80–81 of your Success Guide.

FURTHER LENGTH, AREA AND VOLUME

A

Choose just one answer, a, b, c or d.

1. A sphere has a radius of 3 cm. What is the volume of the sphere given in terms of π?
   a) 12π b) 36π c) 42π d) $\frac{81}{4}\pi$

   (1 mark)

2. A sphere has a radius of 4 cm. What is the surface area of the sphere, given in terms of π?
   a) 64π b) 32π
   c) $\frac{256}{3}\pi$ d) 25π (1 mark)

3. The volume of a pyramid is 25 cm³. The area of the base is 12 cm². What is the perpendicular height of the pyramid?
   a) 7.2 cm b) 4 cm
   c) 25 cm   d) 6.25 cm

   (1 mark)

Questions 4 and 5 refer to the diagram opposite.

(Diagram: circle with centre O, radius 6 cm, angle AOB = 50°)

4. What is the length of arc AOB?
   a) 5.2 cm b) 5.8 cm
   c) 6.2 cm d) 7.4 cm   (1 mark)

5. What is the area of sector AOB?
   a) 15.2 cm² b) 25.3 cm²
   c) 15.7 cm² d) 16.9 cm²

   (1 mark)

Score / 5

B

Answer all parts of the questions.

1. The volumes of the solids below have been calculated. Match the correct solid with the correct volume.

   A: cone, height 12 cm, base radius 5 cm
   B: cylinder with hemisphere top, height 4.3 cm, diameter 10 cm
   C: sphere, diameter 8 cm
   D: pyramid, height 9.7 cm, base 4.2 cm × 5 cm

   600 cm³ .... 68 cm³ .... 314 cm³ .... 2145 cm³ ....
   (2 marks)   (2 marks)   (2 marks)   (2 marks)

2. Decide whether this statement is true or false.

   You must show sufficient working in order to justify your answer.

   'The area of the shaded segment is 3.26 cm²'

   (Diagram: circle with centre O, radius 5 cm, angle AOB = 60°, segment shaded)

   ....
   ....
   ....
   (3 marks)

Score / 11

C These are GCSE style questions. Answer all parts of the questions. Show your workings (on separate paper if necessary) and include the correct units in your answers.

1 The sector area of a circle is 51.6 cm².

The radius of the circle is 9 cm.

Work out the size of the angle θ of the sector.

Give your answer to the nearest degree.

....

....

....

.... °

(3 marks)

Area = 51.6 cm²
9 cm
θ

2 The diagram shows a plastic container.

The container is formed by joining a cylindrical tube to a hemisphere.

The diameter of the cylinder and hemisphere is 26 cm.

The total height of the container is 51 cm.

Work out the volume of the container.

Give your answer correct to 3 significant figures.

....

....

....

.... m³

(4 marks)

51 cm
26 cm

3 The volume of a ball bearing is 268 mm³.

Work out the diameter of the ball bearing, giving your answer to the nearest whole number.

....

....

....

.... mm

(3 marks)

Score   / 10

How well did you do?
1–7 marks   Try again
8–12 marks Getting there
3–19 marks Good work
20–26 marks Excellent!

TOTAL SCORE   / 26

For more information on this topic see pages 82–83 of your Success Guide.

VECTORS

A
Choose just one answer, a, b, c or d.

1. If vector $\underline{a} = \begin{pmatrix} 2 \\ 3 \end{pmatrix}$ and vector $\underline{b} = \begin{pmatrix} -5 \\ -2 \end{pmatrix}$, what is $\underline{a} + \underline{b}$?
   a) $\begin{pmatrix} 1 \\ -3 \end{pmatrix}$
   b) $\begin{pmatrix} -3 \\ 1 \end{pmatrix}$
   c) $\begin{pmatrix} 7 \\ -5 \end{pmatrix}$
   d) $\begin{pmatrix} -10 \\ -6 \end{pmatrix}$ (1 mark)

2. If vector $\underline{c} = \begin{pmatrix} -4 \\ 2 \end{pmatrix}$ and vector $\underline{d} = \begin{pmatrix} -2 \\ -7 \end{pmatrix}$, what is $\underline{c} - \underline{d}$?
   a) $\begin{pmatrix} 8 \\ -14 \end{pmatrix}$
   b) $\begin{pmatrix} -6 \\ -5 \end{pmatrix}$
   c) $\begin{pmatrix} -2 \\ 9 \end{pmatrix}$
   d) $\begin{pmatrix} -6 \\ 5 \end{pmatrix}$ (1 mark)

3. If vector $\underline{p} = \begin{pmatrix} 7 \\ -2 \end{pmatrix}$ and vector $\underline{r} = \begin{pmatrix} -9 \\ 2 \end{pmatrix}$, what is $4\underline{p} + \underline{r}$?
   a) $\begin{pmatrix} 19 \\ -6 \end{pmatrix}$
   b) $\begin{pmatrix} 38 \\ 0 \end{pmatrix}$
   c) $\begin{pmatrix} -6 \\ 19 \end{pmatrix}$
   d) $\begin{pmatrix} 20 \\ -3 \end{pmatrix}$ (1 mark)

4. If vector $\underline{t} = \begin{pmatrix} 3 \\ -2 \end{pmatrix}$, what is the magnitude of $\underline{t}$?
   a) $\sqrt{5}$
   b) $\sqrt{10}$
   c) 13
   d) $\sqrt{13}$ (1 mark)

5. Which vector is parallel to vector $\underline{r} = \begin{pmatrix} -4 \\ 6 \end{pmatrix}$?
   a) $\begin{pmatrix} -8 \\ 6 \end{pmatrix}$
   b) $\begin{pmatrix} -16 \\ 24 \end{pmatrix}$
   c) $\begin{pmatrix} -4 \\ 12 \end{pmatrix}$
   d) $\begin{pmatrix} -8 \\ 18 \end{pmatrix}$ (1 mark)

Score / 5

B
Answer all parts of the questions.

1. The questions below refer to the diagram opposite.

   Decide whether the statements are true or false.

   a) $\vec{OB} = a + b$ ....
   b) $\vec{BC} = -a + b + c$ ....
   c) $\vec{AC} = -a + c$ ....
   d) If N is the midpoint of OC then $\vec{AN} = -\frac{1}{2}c + a$ .... (4 marks)

2. If $\vec{OC} = 2a - 3b$ and $\vec{OD} = 12a - 18b$, write down two geometrical facts about the vectors $\vec{OC}$ and $\vec{OD}$.

   ....
   .... (2 marks)

3. On the grid below draw the vectors **a** and **b** and complete the statement.

   a) $a = \begin{pmatrix} 3 \\ 2 \end{pmatrix}$, $b = \begin{pmatrix} -4 \\ 6 \end{pmatrix}$ $a + b = \begin{pmatrix} \ \end{pmatrix}$

   b) $a = \begin{pmatrix} 1 \\ 4 \end{pmatrix}$, $b = \begin{pmatrix} -2 \\ 5 \end{pmatrix}$ $a - b = \begin{pmatrix} \ \end{pmatrix}$

(4 marks)

Score / 10

C These are GCSE style questions. Answer all parts of the questions. Show your workings (on separate paper if necessary) and include the correct units in your answers.

1

$\vec{OA} = 3\mathbf{a}$, $\vec{OB} = 3\mathbf{b}$, $\vec{OC} = 5\mathbf{a}$, $\vec{BD} = 2\mathbf{b}$

Prove that AB is parallel to CD.

....

.... (3 marks)

2

ABCD is a quadrilateral with $\vec{AB} = \mathbf{a}$, $\vec{BC} = \mathbf{b}$ and $\vec{CD} = 2\mathbf{b} - \mathbf{a}$.

a) Express $\vec{AC}$ in terms of **a** and **b**. .... (1 mark)

b) Prove that BC is parallel to AD. .... (2 marks)

c) N is the midpoint of CD.

Express $\vec{AN}$ in terms of **a** and **b**.

....

.... (2 marks)

d) Y is the point on AN such that AY : YN = 3 : 1

Show that $\vec{YD} = \frac{3}{8}(4\mathbf{b} - \mathbf{a})$.

....

.... (3 marks)

Score   / 11

How well did you do?
1–4 marks Try again
5–9 marks Getting there
10–17 marks Good work
18–26 marks Excellent!

TOTAL SCORE   / 26

For more information on this topic see pages 84–85 of your Success Guide.

COLLECTING DATA

A Choose just one answer, a, b, c or d.

1. What is the name given to data you collect yourself?
   a) continuous
   b) primary
   c) secondary
   d) discrete
   (1 mark)

2. Data which is usually obtained by counting is said to be this type of data.
   a) continuous
   b) primary
   c) secondary
   d) discrete
   (1 mark)

3. This type of data changes from one category to the next.
   a) continuous
   b) primary
   c) secondary
   d) discrete
   (1 mark)

4. This type of data gives a word as an answer.
   a) quantitative
   b) qualitative
   c) continuous
   d) discrete
   (1 mark)

5. A survey is being carried out on the number of hours some students spend watching television. In year 7 there were 240 students, year 8 has 300 and year 9 460 students. John decides to use a stratified sample of 100 students. How many students should he ask from year 7?
   a) 46
   b) 30
   c) 48
   d) 24
   (1 mark)

Score / 5

B Answer all parts of the questions.

1. Jim and Annabelle are designing a survey to use in the school. One of their questions is shown below.

   How much time do you spend doing homework per night?   0–1 hrs   1–2 hrs   2–3 hrs   3–4 hrs

   What is the problem with this question? Rewrite the question so that it is improved.

   ....

   ....

   .... (2 marks)

2. Laura conducts a survey of the students in her school. She decides to interview 100 students.

   Calculate the number of students she should choose from each year group to provide a representative sample. Complete the table below.

Year group	Number of students	Number of students in sample
7	120	
8	176	
9	160	
10	190	
11	154	

   (3 marks)

   Score / 5

C These are GCSE style questions. Answer all parts of the questions. Show your workings (on separate paper if necessary) and include the correct units in your answers.

1 Mrs Robinson is going to sell chocolate bars at the school tuck shop. She wants to know what type of chocolate bars pupils like. Design a suitable questionnaire she could use.

(2 marks)

2 Robert is conducting a survey into television habits. One of the questions in his survey is: 'Do you watch a lot of television?'.

His friend Jessica tells him that it is not a very good question. Write down two ways in which Robert could improve the question.

....

....

....

....

(2 marks)

3 The table shows the gender and number of students in each year group.

Year group	Number of boys	Number of girls	Total
7	160	120	280
8	108	132	240
9	158	117	275
10	85	70	155
11	140	110	250

Mark is carrying out a survey about how much pocket money students are given.

He decides to take a stratified sample of 150 students from the whole school.

Calculate how many in the stratified sample should be:

a) students from Year 8 .... students

b) girls from Year 11 .... girls

(4 marks)

Score / 8

How well did you do?
1–4 marks   Try again
5–9 marks   Getting there
10–13 marks   Good work
14–18 marks   Excellent!

TOTAL SCORE   / 18

For more information on this topic see pages 88–89 of your Success Guide.

SCATTER DIAGRAMS AND CORRELATION

A

Choose just one answer, a, b, c or d.

1 A scatter diagram is drawn to show the height and weight of some students. What type of correlation is shown?

a) zero
b) negative
c) positive
d) scattered

(1 mark)

2 A scatter diagram is drawn to show the maths score and the height of a group of students. What type of correlation is shown?

a) zero
b) negative
c) positive
d) scattered

(1 mark)

3 A scatter diagram is drawn to show the age of some cars and their values. What type of correlation would be shown?

a) zero   b) negative
c) positive   d) scattered   (1 mark)

Score   / 3

B

Answer all parts of the questions.

1 Some statements have been written on cards.

[Positive Correlation]   [Negative Correlation]   [No Correlation]

Decide which card best describes these relationships.

a) The temperature and the sales of ice lollies .... (1 mark)

b) The temperature and the sales of woollen gloves .... (1 mark)

c) The weight of a person and his waist measurement .... (1 mark)

d) The height of a person and his IQ .... (1 mark)

2 The scatter diagram shows the marks scored in a Mathematics and Physics examination.

a) Describe the relationship between the Mathematics and Physics scores.

.... (1 mark)

b) Draw a line of best fit on the scatter diagram.   (1 mark)

c) Use your line of best fit to estimate the Mathematics score that Jonathan is likely to obtain if he has a Physics score of 75%.

.... (1 mark)

Score   / 7

76

C These are GCSE style questions. Answer all parts of the questions. Show your workings (on separate paper if necessary) and include the correct units in your answers.

1 The table shows the ages of some children and the total number of hours sleep they had between noon on Saturday and noon on Sunday.

Age (years)	2	6	5	3	12	9	2	10	5	10	7	11	12	3
No. of hours sleep	15	13.1	13.2	14.8	10.1	11.8	15.6	11.6	13.5	11.8	12.8	10.2	9.5	14

a) On the scatter diagram, plot the information from the table.

(4 marks)

b) Describe the correlation between the age of the children in years and the total number of hours sleep they had.

....

.... (2 marks)

c) Draw a line of best fit on your diagram. (1 mark)

d) Estimate the total number of hours sleep for a 4-year-old child.

.... (2 marks)

e) Explain why the line of best fit only gives an estimate for the number of hours slept.

....

.... (2 marks)

Score / 11

How well did you do?
1–4 marks   Try again
5–10 marks Getting there
11–15 marks Good work
16–21 marks Excellent!

TOTAL SCORE   / 21

For more on this topic see pages 92–93 of your Success Guide.

SCATTER DIAGRAMS AND CORRELATION

AVERAGES 1

A Choose just one answer, a, b, c or d.

1. What is the mean of this set of data?
 2, 7, 1, 4, 2, 6, 2, 5, 2, 6
 a) 4.2
 b) 3.6
 c) 3.7
 d) 3.9 (1 mark)

2. What is the median value of the set of data used in question 1?
 a) 2
 b) 3
 c) 4
 d) 5 (1 mark)

3. What is the range of this set of data?
 2, 7, 1, 4, 11, 9, 6
 a) 1
 b) 6
 c) 11
 d) 10 (1 mark)

4. A die is thrown and the scores are noted. The results are shown in the table below. What is the mean die score?

Die score	1	2	3	4	5	6
Frequency	12	15	10	8	14	13

 a) 5
 b) 3
 c) 4
 d) 3.5 (1 mark)

5. Using the information in the table above, what is the modal score?
 a) 15
 b) 2
 c) 4
 d) 8 (1 mark)

Score / 5

B Answer all parts of the questions.

1. Here are some number cards.

 8, 7, 11, 4, 2, 1, 3, 12, 4, 4

 Decide whether the following statements, which refer to the number cards above, are true or false.

 a) The range of the number cards is 1–11. .... (1 mark)
 b) The mean of the number cards is 5.6. .... (1 mark)
 c) The median of the number cards is 5. .... (1 mark)
 d) The mode of the number cards is 4. .... (1 mark)

2. A baked beans factory claims that 'on average, a tin of baked beans contains 141 beans'.

 In order to check the accuracy of this claim a sample of 20 tins was taken and the number of beans in each tin counted.

Number of beans	137	138	139	140	141	142	143	144
Number of tins	1	1	1	2	5	4	4	2

 a) Calculate the mean number of beans per tin. .... (2 marks)
 b) Explain briefly whether you think the manufacturer is justified in making its claim.
 .... (1 mark)

3. The mean of 7, 9, 10, 18, x and 17 is 13. What is the value of x? .... (2 marks)

Score / 9

C These are GCSE style questions. Answer all parts of the questions. Show your workings (on separate paper if necessary) and include the correct units in your answers.

1 Some students took a test. The table gives information about their marks in the test.

Mark	Frequency
3	2
4	5
5	11
6	2

Work out the mean mark.

....

.... (3 marks)

2 Simon has sat three examinations. His mean score is 65. To pass the unit, he needs to get an average of 69. What score must he get in the final examination to pass the unit?

....

.... (3 marks)

3 A company employs 3 women and 7 men.

The mean weekly wage of the 10 employees is £464.

The mean weekly wage of the 3 women is £520.

Calculate the mean weekly wage of the 7 men.

....

.... (4 marks)

4 Find the three point moving average for the following data

  2   5   3   6   2   1   4

....

....

....

.... (5 marks)

Score / 15

How well did you do?
1–10 marks   Try again
11–16 marks Getting there
17–22 marks Good work
23–29 marks Excellent!

TOTAL SCORE   / 29

For more information on this topic see pages 94–95 of your Success Guide.

AVERAGES 2

A
Choose just one answer, a, b, c or d.

The following questions are based on the information given in the table below about the time taken in seconds to swim 50 metres.

Time (seconds)	Frequency (f)
$0 \leq t < 30$	1
$30 \leq t < 60$	2
$60 \leq t < 90$	4
$90 \leq t < 120$	6
$120 \leq t < 150$	7
$150 \leq t < 180$	2

1 How many people swam 50 metres in less than 60 seconds?
a) 2 b) 4 c) 3 d) 6 (1 mark)

2 Which of the intervals is the modal class?
a) $60 \leq t < 90$ b) $120 \leq t < 150$
c) $30 \leq t < 60$ d) $90 \leq t < 120$ (1 mark)

3 Which of the class intervals contains the median value?
a) $90 \leq t < 120$ b) $150 \leq t < 180$
c) $120 \leq t < 150$ d) $60 \leq t < 90$ (1 mark)

4 What is the estimate for the mean time to swim 50 metres?
a) 105 seconds b) 385 seconds
c) 100 seconds d) 125 seconds (1 mark)

Score / 4

B
Answer all parts of the questions.

1 The length of some seedlings are shown in the table below.

Length in mm	Number of seedlings
$0 \leq L < 10$	3
$10 \leq L < 20$	5
$20 \leq L < 30$	9
$30 \leq L < 40$	2
$40 \leq L < 50$	1

Calculate an estimate for the mean length of the seedlings.

Mean = ... mm (4 marks)

2 The stem and leaf diagram shows the marks gained by some students in a mathematics examination.

Stem	Leaf
1	2 5 7
2	6 9
3	4 5 5 7
4	2 7 7 7 7
5	2

Stem = 10 marks

Key: 1|2 = 12 marks

Using the stem and leaf diagram calculate:

a) the mode. .... (1 mark)

b) the median. .... (1 mark)

c) the range. .... (1 mark)

Score / 7

C These are GCSE style questions. Answer all parts of the questions. Show your workings (on separate paper if necessary) and include the correct units in your answers.

1 A psychologist records the time, to the nearest minute, taken by 20 students to complete a logic problem.

Here are the results.

| 12 | 22 | 31 | 36 | 35 | 14 | 27 | 23 | 19 | 25 |
| 15 | 17 | 15 | 27 | 32 | 38 | 41 | 18 | 27 | 18 |

Draw a stem and leaf diagram to show this information.

(4 marks)

2 John asks 100 people how much they spent last year on newspapers. The results are in the table below.

Amount £ (x)	Frequency
$0 \leq x < 10$	12
$10 \leq x < 20$	20
$20 \leq x < 30$	15
$30 \leq x < 40$	18
$40 \leq x < 50$	14
$50 \leq x < 60$	18
$60 \leq x < 70$	3

a) Calculate an estimate of the mean amount spent on newspapers.

.... (4 marks)

b) Explain briefly why this value of the mean is only an estimate.

.... (1 mark)

c) Calculate the class interval in which the median lies.

.... (2 marks)

Score / 11

How well did you do?
1–6 marks   Try again
7–11 marks Getting there
12–16 marks Good work
17–22 marks Excellent!

TOTAL SCORE   / 22

For more information on this topic see pages 96–97 of your Success Guide.

CUMULATIVE FREQUENCY GRAPHS

A

Choose just one answer, a, b, c or d.

The data below shows the number of letters delivered to each of the 15 houses in Whelan Avenue (arranged in order of size).
0, 0, 1, 1, 1, 1, 1, 1, 2, 2, 2, 3, 4, 5, 5

Use the information above to answer these questions.

1 What is the median number of letters delivered?
a) 0
b) 2
c) 1
d) 5 (1 mark)

2 What is the lower quartile for the number of letters delivered?
a) 0
b) 2
c) 3
d) 1 (1 mark)

3 What is the upper quartile for the number of letters delivered?
a) 0
b) 2
c) 3
d) 1 (1 mark)

4 What is the interquartile range for the number of letters delivered?
a) 2
b) 3
c) 4
d) 5 (1 mark)

Score / 4

B

Answer all parts of the questions.

1 The table shows the examination marks of some year 10 pupils in their end of year mathematics examination.

Examination mark	Frequency	Cumulative frequency
0–10	4	
11–20	6	
21–30	11	
31–40	24	
41–50	18	
51–60	7	
61–70	3	

a) Complete the cumulative frequency column in the table above. (2 marks)

b) Draw the cumulative frequency graph. (3 marks)

c) From your graph, find the median mark. .... (1 mark)

d) From your graph, find the interquartile range. .... (2 marks)

e) If 16 pupils were given a grade A in the examination, what is the minimum score needed for a grade A?

.... marks (2 marks)

Score / 10

C These are GCSE style questions. Answer all parts of the questions. Show your workings (on separate paper if necessary) and include the correct units in your answers.

1 The table gives information about the time, to the nearest minute, taken to run a marathon.

Time (nearest minute)	Frequency	Cumulative frequency
$120 < t \leq 140$	1	
$140 < t \leq 160$	8	
$160 < t \leq 180$	24	
$180 < t \leq 200$	29	
$200 < t \leq 220$	10	
$220 < t \leq 240$	5	
$240 < t \leq 260$	3	

a) Complete the table to show the cumulative frequency for this data. (2 marks)

b) Draw the cumulative frequency graph for the data.

(3 marks)

c) Use your graph to work out an estimate for these.

 i) The interquartile range. .... minutes (2 marks)

 i) The number of runners with a time of more than 205 minutes.

 .... runners (1 mark)

d) Draw a box plot for this data.

(3 marks)

Score / 11

How well did you do?
1–6 marks Try again
7–12 marks Getting there
13–18 marks Good work
19–25 marks Excellent!

TOTAL SCORE / 25

For more information on this topic see pages 98–99 of your Success Guide.

HISTOGRAMS

A

Choose just one answer, a, b, c or d.

The table shows the distance travelled to work by some employees. Use the information in the table to answer the questions below.

Distance (km)	Frequency
$0 \leq d < 5$	8
$5 \leq d < 15$	20
$15 \leq d < 20$	135
$20 \leq d < 30$	47
$30 \leq d < 50$	80

1 Which class interval has a frequency density of 4.7?
  a) $0 \leq d < 5$ b) $5 \leq d < 15$
  c) $15 \leq d < 20$ d) $20 \leq d < 30$ (1 mark)

2 The frequency density for one of the class intervals is 4. Which one?
  a) $5 \leq d < 15$ b) $30 \leq d < 50$
  c) $0 \leq d < 5$ d) $15 \leq d < 20$
  (1 mark)

3 Which class interval has the highest frequency density?
  a) $0 \leq d < 5$ b) $15 \leq d < 20$
  c) $20 \leq d < 30$ d) $5 \leq d < 15$
  (1 mark)

4 Which class interval has the lowest frequency density?
  a) $0 \leq d < 5$ b) $5 \leq d < 15$
  c) $15 \leq d < 20$ d) $30 \leq d < 50$
  (1 mark)

Score / 4

B

Answer all parts of the questions.

1 The table and histogram give information about how long, in minutes, some students took to complete a maths problem.

Time (in minutes)	Frequency
$0 < t \leq 5$	19
$5 < t \leq 15$	....
$15 < t \leq 20$	16
$20 < t \leq 30$	....
$30 < t \leq 45$	12

a) Use the information in the histogram to complete the table.   (2 marks)

b) Use the table to complete the histogram.   (2 marks)

Score / 4

C These are GCSE style questions. Answer all parts of the questions. Show your workings (on separate paper if necessary) and include the correct units in your answers.

1. The weights of some objects are given in the table below.

Weight W (kg)	Frequency
$0 \leq W < 2$	14
$2 \leq W < 3$	8
$3 \leq W < 5$	13
$5 \leq W < 10$	14
$10 \leq W < 12$	7
$W \geq 12$	0

Draw a histogram to show the distribution of the weights of the objects. Use a scale of 2 cm to 2 kg on the weight axis.

(3 marks)

2. Pierre recorded the length, in seconds, of some advertisements shown on television in a week.

His results are shown in the histogram.

Use the information in the histogram to complete the table.

Length S (in seconds)	Frequency
$0 \leq S < 10$	....
$10 \leq S < 15$	....
$15 \leq S < 20$	21
$20 \leq S < 40$	....
$S \geq 40$	0

(3 marks)

Score / 6

How well did you do?
1–2 marks   Try again
3–6 marks   Getting there
7–10 marks   Good work
11–14 marks Excellent!

TOTAL SCORE   / 14

For more information on this topic see page 100 of your Success Guide.

PROBABILITY

A Choose just one answer, a, b, c or d.

1. The probability that Highbury football club win a football match is $\frac{12}{17}$. What is the probability that they do not win the football match?
   a) $\frac{5}{12}$
   b) $\frac{17}{29}$
   c) $\frac{12}{17}$
   d) $\frac{5}{17}$ (1 mark)

2. A fair die is thrown 600 times. On how many of these throws would you expect to get a 4?
   a) 40
   b) 600
   c) 100
   d) 580 (1 mark)

3. A fair die is thrown 500 times. If a 6 comes up 87 times, what is the relative frequency?
   a) $\frac{1}{6}$
   b) $\frac{87}{500}$
   c) $\frac{10}{600}$
   d) $\frac{1}{587}$ (1 mark)

4. The probability that it snows on Christmas day is 0.2. What is the probability that it will snow on Christmas day in two consecutive years?
   a) 0.04
   b) 0.4
   c) 0.2
   d) 0.16 (1 mark)

5. The probability that Fiona is in the hockey team is 0.7. The probability that she is picked for the netball team is 0.3. What is the probability that she is picked for both teams?
   a) 1.0
   b) 0.1
   c) 0.12
   d) 0.21 (1 mark)

Score / 5

B Answer all parts of the questions.

1. Two spinners are spun at the same time and their scores are added.

   Spinner 1: 3, 3, 2, 1
   Spinner 2: 6, 2, 3, 1

   a) Complete the sample space diagrams to show the outcomes.

Spinner 2 \ Spinner 1	1	2	3	3
1	2			
2		4		
3		5		
6		8		9

   (2 marks)

   b) Find the probability of:
      i) a score of 4. ....
      ii) a score of 9. ....
      iii) a score of 1. .... (3 marks)

2. The probability that Michelle finishes first in a swimming race is 0.3. Michelle swims two races; work out the probability that Michelle wins both races. .... (2 marks)

3. There are 13 counters in a bag: 7 are red and the rest are white. A counter is picked at random, its colour noted and then it is replaced. A second counter is then chosen. What is the probability of choosing:

   a) Two red counters? .... (2 marks)

   b) A red and a white counter? .... (3 marks)

Score / 12

C These are GCSE style questions. Answer all parts of the questions. Show your workings (on separate paper if necessary) and include the correct units in your answers.

1 A bag contains different coloured beads.

The probability of taking a bead of a particular colour at random is as follows.

Colour	Red	White	Blue	Pink
Probability	0.25	0.1		0.3

Jackie is going to take a bead at random and then put it back in the bag.

a) i) Work out the probability that Jackie will take out a blue bead. .... (1 mark)

ii) Write down the probability that Jackie will take out a black bead. .... (1 mark)

b) Jackie will take out a bead from the bag at random 200 times, replacing the bead each time. Work out an estimate for the number of times that Jackie takes a red bead.

.... (2 marks)

2 Two fair dice are thrown together and their scores are added.

a) Work out the probability of a score of 7. .... (2 marks)

b) Work out the probability of a score of 9. .... (2 marks)

3 Kevin and Nathan challenge each other to a game of Monopoly and a game of pool.
A draw is not possible in either game.

The probability that Kevin wins at Monopoly is 0.4

The probability that Nathan wins at pool is 0.7

a) Draw a probability tree diagram in the space below.

(3 marks)

b) What is the probability that Nathan wins both games? .... (2 marks)

c) What is the probability that they win a game each? .... (3 marks)

Score / 16

How well did you do?
1–11 marks Try again
12–21 marks Getting there
22–27 marks Good work
28–33 marks Excellent!

TOTAL SCORE / 33

For more information on this topic see pages 102–105 of your Success Guide.

NOTES

MIXED GCSE-STYLE QUESTIONS

Answer these questions. Show full working out.

1 Here are the first four terms of an arithmetic sequence.

5, 9, 13, 17

Find an expression, in terms of n, for the nth term of the sequence.

.... (2 marks)

2 The diagram shows the position of three towns, A, B and C. Town C is due east of towns A and B. Town B is due east of A.

```
•————————————•———•
A             B   C
```

Town B is $3\frac{1}{3}$ miles from town A.

Town C is $1\frac{1}{4}$ miles from town B.

Calculate the number of miles between town A and town C.

.... (3 marks)

3 a) Solve $5x - 2 = 3(x + 6)$ $x = $ .... (2 marks)

b) Solve $\dfrac{3 - 2x}{4} = 2$ $x = $ .... (2 marks)

c) i) Factorise $x^2 - 10x + 24$ .... (2 marks)

    ii) Hence solve $x^2 - 10x + 24$ .... (1 mark)

d) Simplify $\dfrac{x^2 + 2x}{x^2 + 5x + 6}$ .... (3 marks)

e) Simplify these.

   i) $p^4 \times p^6$ .... (1 mark)

   ii) $\dfrac{p^7}{p^3}$ .... (1 mark)

   iii) $\dfrac{p^4 \times p^5}{p}$ .... (1 mark)

   iv) $(p^{-\frac{1}{2}})^4$ .... (1 mark)

4 The times, in minutes, to finish an assault course are listed in order.

8, 12, 12, 13, 15, 17, 22, 23, 23, 27, 29

a) Find:

   i) the lower quartile ....

   ii) the interquartile range .... (2 marks)

b) Draw a box plot for this data.

(3 marks)

5 a) Megan bought a TV for £700. Each year the TV depreciated by 20%.

Work out the value of the TV two years after she bought it.

.... (3 marks)

b) In a '20% off' sale, William bought a DVD player for £300. What was the original price of the DVD player before the sale?

.... (3 marks)

6 The diagram shows a right-angled triangle.

PQ = 14.2 cm.

Angle PRQ = 90°.

Angle RPQ = 38°.

Find the length of the side QR. Give your answer to 3 significant figures.

.... (3 marks)

7 The table gives the times to the nearest minute to complete a puzzle.

Time (nearest min)	Frequency
$0 \leq t < 10$	5
$10 \leq t < 20$	12
$20 \leq t < 30$	8
$30 \leq t < 40$	5

Calculate an estimate for the mean number of minutes to complete the puzzle.

.... (4 marks)

8 a) $b = \dfrac{a + c}{ac}$

$a = 3.2 \times 10^5$

$c = 5 \times 10^6$

Calculate the value of b.

Give your answer in standard form.. .... (2 marks)

b) Rearrange the formula to make a the subject. .... (2 marks)

9

D, B and C are points on a circle with centre O.

AB and AC are tangents to the circle. Angle ACB = 72°.

a) Explain why angle OCB is 18°.

....

.... (1 mark)

b) Calculate the size of angle BDC. Give reasons for your answer.

....

....

.... (3 marks)

91

10 The diagram shows the graphs of these equations.

$x + y = 4$

$y = x - 2$

a) Use the diagram to solve the simultaneous equations

$x + y = 4$ $x = $ ....

$y + 2 = x$ $y = $ ....   (4 marks)

b) On the grid, shade in the region satisfied by these inequalities.

$x + y \leq 4$

$y \geq x - 2$ (2 marks)

11 a) The number 360 can be written as $2^a \times 3^b \times 5^c$

Calculate the values of a, b and c.

.... (3 marks)

b) Find the highest common factor of 56 and 60.

.... (2 marks)

c) Find the lowest common multiple of 56 and 60.

.... (2 marks)

12 a) p is an integer such that $0 < 4p \leq 13$

List all the possible values of p.

.... (1 mark)

b) Solve the inequality $\dfrac{t + 1}{4} \leq t - 3$

.... (2 marks)

13 $a = 2 + \sqrt{7}$ and $b = 2 - 3\sqrt{7}$

Simplify the following, giving your answer in the form $p + q\sqrt{7}$, where p and q are integers.

a) $a + b$ .... (3 marks)

b) a^2 .... (3 marks)

c) ab .... (3 marks)

14

PQRS is a cyclic quadrilateral.

PS = 4.3 cm, SR = 2.7 cm, angle PSR = 143° and PQ = QR.

a) Calculate the length of PR. .... cm (3 marks)

b) Calculate the length of QR. .... cm (3 marks)

c) Calculate the area of triangle PQR. .... cm² (3 marks)

15 Solve the equation $\dfrac{x-4}{x^2-16} + \dfrac{2}{2x-4} = 1$

Leave your answers in surd form. $x = $ .... (5 marks)

16 The diagram shows a child's toy, which is hollow. The height of the cone is 4 cm. The base radius of cone and hemisphere is 3 cm.

a) Work out the total surface area of the toy.

Give your answer as a multiple of π.

.... cm²   (4 marks)

b) The toy is made in two sizes. The large toy is three times the size of the toy above.

What is the total surface area of the large toy? Give your answer as a multiple of π.

.... cm²   (3 marks)

17

A triangular piece of metal is cut out of a rectangular piece of metal.

The length of the rectangle is $2x + 4$ cm

The width of the rectangle is $x + 6$ cm

The height of the triangle is $x + 4$ cm

The base of the triangle is $x + 1$ cm

The shaded region in the diagram shows the metal remaining.

The area of the shaded region is 38.5 cm².

a) Show that $x^2 + 9x - 11 = 0$.

....

.... (4 marks)

b) i) Solve the equation $x^2 + 9x - 11 = 0$.

Give your answer correct to 3 significant figures.

.... (3 marks)

ii) Hence find the area of the triangle.

.... (1 mark)

18 Riddlington High School is holding a sponsored walk. The pupils at the school decide whether or not to take part. The probability that Afshan will take part is $\frac{2}{3}$. The probability that Bethany will take part is $\frac{4}{5}$ and the probability that Colin with take part is $\frac{1}{4}$.

Calculate the probability that:

a) all three take part in the sponsored walk

.... (2 marks)

b) exactly two of them take part in the sponsored walk

.... (3 marks)

Mixed questions answers

1 $4n + 1$

2 $4\frac{7}{12}$ miles

3 **a)** $x = 10$ **b)** $x = -2.5$ **c)** i) $(x-4)(x-6)$
  ii) $x = 4$ and $x = 6$

  d) $\dfrac{x(x+2)}{(x+2)(x+3)} = \dfrac{x}{x+3}$ **e)** i) p^{10} ii) p^4
  iii) p^8 iv) $p^{-2} = \dfrac{1}{p^2}$

4 **a)** i) lower quartile = 12

  ii) interquartile range = 11

  b) [box plot showing data from approximately 7 to 28, with box from 12 to 23 and median at 18]

5 **a)** £448 **b)** £375

6 8.74 cm

7 $19.\dot{3}$ minutes

8 **a)** 3.325×10^{-6} **b)** $a = \dfrac{c}{bc - 1}$

9 **a)** The radius and tangent meet at 90°.
  Since angle ACB = 72° then angle OCB = 90° − 72° = 18°.

  b) Angle OCB = angle OBC = 18°. Angle BOC = 180° − (2 × 18°) = 144°.

  Angle BDC = 144° ÷ 2, since the angle subtended at the centre is twice the angle at the circumference.

  Angle BDC = 72°.

10 **a)** $x = 3$
  $y = 1$

  b) [graph showing lines $x = y - 2$ and $x + y = 4$ with shaded region]

11 a) $a = 3, b = 2, c = 1$ b) 4   c) 840
12 a) 1, 2, 3   b) $t \geq 13/3$
13 a) $4 - 2\sqrt{7}$ b) $11 + 4\sqrt{7}$ c) $-17 - 4\sqrt{7}$
14 a) 6.66 cm (3 s.f.)   b) 10.49 cm (3 s.f.)   c) 33.1 cm^2 (3 s.f.)

15
$$\frac{x-4}{x^2-16} + \frac{2}{2x-4} = 1$$

$$\frac{x-4}{(x-4)(x+4)} + \frac{2}{2(x-2)} = 1$$

$$\frac{1}{(x+4)} + \frac{1}{(x-2)} = 1$$

$x - 2 + x + 4 = 1\ (x+4)(x-2)$

$2x + 2 = x^2 + 2x - 8$

$x^2 + 2x - 8 - 2x - 2 = 0$

$x^2 - 10 = 0$

$x = \pm\sqrt{10}$

$x = +\sqrt{10}$ or $x = -\sqrt{10}$

16 a) Curved surface area of cone = $\pi r l$

$\pi \times 3 \times 5 = 15\pi$

Curved surface area of hemisphere = $\frac{4\pi r^2}{2}$

$2\pi \times 9 = 18\pi$

Total curved surface area = 33π

b) Linear scale factor = 3

Area scale factor = $3^2 = 9$

Curved surface area of larger toy = 297π

17 a) $(2x+4)(x+6) - \frac{1}{2} \times (x+1)(x+4) = 38.5$

$2x^2 + 16x + 24 - \frac{(x^2 + 5x + 4)}{2} = 38.5$

$4x^2 + 32x + 48 - x^2 - 5x - 4 = 77$

$3x^2 + 27x + 44 = 77$

$3x^2 + 27x - 33 = 0$

$(\div 3) \therefore x^2 + 9x - 11 = 0$

b) i) $x = 1.09$ or $x = -10.09$, but $x > 0$

ii) Area of triangle = $\frac{1}{2} \times 2.09 \times 5.09$

= 5.319 05

= 5.32 cm^2 (3 s.f.)

18 a) $\frac{2}{15}$ b) $\frac{1}{2}$